RAMSAY, Jimmy

The Killers

THE KILLERS

VAGABONDS & VICTIMS

by jimmy ramsay

Independent Music Press

Published in 2005 by
INDEPENDENT MUSIC PRESS
Independent Music Press is an imprint of I.M. P. Publishing Limited
This Work is Copyright © I. M. P. Publishing Ltd 2005

The Killers: Vagabonds & Victims by Jimmy Ramsay

British Library Cataloguing-in-Publication Data.
A catalogue for this book is available from The British Library.

ISBN 0-9549704-2-X

Cover Design by Fresh Lemon.
Edited by Martin Roach.

Printed and bound in the UK by Bookmarque Ltd

Independent Music Press
P.O. Box 69, Church Stretton, Shropshire SY6 6WZ

Visit us on the web at: www.impbooks.com

For a free catalogue, e-mail us at: info@impbooks.com
Fax: 01694 720049

Acknowledgements:

Many thanks to the following for helping me with this book: Darren Haynes at The Official Chart Company – all statistics reproduced with kind permission of OCC; the finest article on The Killers to date is by Stuart Clark for *Hot Press* magazine; the team at Starbucks M. Brace, for the gallons of coffee; and Emily and James Dunn.

Dedicated to Mrs Ramsay and A. B. Ramsay.

Prologue:

"Our main selling point really is that we are the greatest band ever to have come out of Las Vegas."

Brandon Flowers, September 2005.

INTRODUCTION

"He's bit his ear off. His ear. Clean off."

I couldn't quite comprehend what the man next to me was saying but as the whispers swirled around the auditorium at Caesar's Palace in Las Vegas, the reality began to sink in. Mike Tyson had bitten a chunk out of Evander Holyfield's ear. Tyson, the former undisputed world heavyweight champion, exhausted from a three-round battering from a born-again Christian with a neck the size of a bull's and a heart to match, had resorted to extreme measures, even for the fight game.

He'd bitten his ear off.

Standing ten rows from the ropes, with Vinnie Jones two seats in front of me and OJ Simpson's celebrity lawyer, the late Johnnie Cochran in between us, I sat back and watched the carnage. What the world's media didn't tell you that night (or the morning after) was that a mini-riot broke out when the contest had finally ended. I saw a huge man in a dinner jacket thrown horizontally over the top rope and into the crowd. Scuffles in the ring and a growing undercurrent of impending violence rippled through the venue.

I decided it was time for my wife and I to leave. Using a back door reserved for 'Catering Staff Only', we slipped out of the mayhem and into the Vegas night. Or what passes for night in a city where there is more neon than Dredd's Mega City Four.

Within sixty minutes of a piece of Holyfield's ear hitting the canvas, I was sitting with my wife in a hotel room inside a black pyramid. We switched the over-sized TV on, flicking past the shopping channels on to the news. The banner headline read 'Vegas Strip Shut Down' amid reports of shootings and fighting on the streets. We hadn't seen any of this. Reporters, anxious to get the scoop, spoke to worried holiday-makers who claimed to have heard gunshots. Others claimed it was merely the sound of rope-barriers falling over in the melee. All I knew was the last time these two boxers had fought in Vegas, Tupac Shakur had gone home in a body bag.

We'd bought the tickets only two hours before the fight for the princely sum of $1000. Ironically, in a hotel the size of a small town that was filled with more frightening looking men than I have ever seen in my entire life, we bought them from two Cockneys. Wide-boys with Arthur Daley accents, bad complexions and snake-eyes. They seemed like the most trust-worthy people there. At one point, I'd lost my petite wife, only to find her talking to a man who must have troubled a seven-foot tape measure, saying, "Got any tickets?"

Gangsters in $5000 bright yellow zoot suits all looked over-sized due to the bullet-proof vests underneath their primary coloured whistles. They mingled genially among scores of scantily-clad 'working ladies'. It was like somebody had sliced through the entire stratum of human life and dumped a slither of each cross-section into this one city. Pimps, hookers, entourages, gangs, loners, freaks, dealers, tourists, touts, pensioners, honeymooners, promoters, press, bell-hops, croupiers, bunny girls ... and us. Surreal, fantastic, frightening, exciting, sordid, glitzy and, above all, unforgettable.

Unforgettable.

It was that kind of night.

Vegas is that kind of city.

The Killers are that kind of band.

It was June 28, 1997. I know because I bought a poster. Back then, The Killers' lead singer Brandon flowers was not yet even working as a bell-hop at one of Vegas's multitude of hotels. Within a few years, he was standing on a stage in Hyde Park singing to a TV audience of three billion. For a band to play in front of that many punters at Hammersmith Appollo would take a gig every night for 2,200 years. The only surprise was that Brandon's band, The Killers, weren't allowed to sing more than one song.

THE KILLERS

Incredible.
He is that kind of frontman.
The Killers are that kind of band.
This is their story.

CHAPTER 1: LAS VEGAS OR MANCHESTER?

"In Vegas, you can be whatever you want to be. You can live a really normal life if you choose, but at the same time, if you want to live a crazy life ... it can be the place for you."
Ronnie Vannucci

When in Europe, Brandon Flowers smokes a cigarette that sounds like a Bavarian condom: Davidoff Gold. He switches to this brand from his usual all-American Marlboro Lights when his band tour on that continent. Unusually for a frontman who is considered a modern sex symbol, this is the extent of his rock and roll excess. His family are Mormon by faith, a belief system that is extremely popular in America, but in the state of Utah in particular (80% of the state are Mormon).

Mormon rock gods are not as rare as you might think. Most notably, perhaps, Wayne Hussey, lead singer with goth giants The Mission was a legendary rock and roller. Such was his band's lifestyle that they even called their live album, *No Snow No Show*, after their own supposed pre-show terms and conditions regarding cocaine.

Such sheer debauchery is – and was – anathema to the

Rock and roll historians are constantly scouring the childhoods and family lives of their chosen subjects to explain away their lyrics, their persona or their careers.

Flowers family. Although Brandon is the only member of The Killers who was actually born in Las Vegas, his family moved from that city to Nephi in Payson, Utah, when he was just eight. Brandon was the youngest child of a family of eight, with one brother and four sisters as siblings.

Rock and roll historians are constantly scouring the childhoods and family lives of their chosen subjects to explain away their lyrics, their persona or their careers. Not so Brandon Flowers. Intriguingly, when questioned about his Mormon faith, Flowers the media star is suddenly less forthcoming. While he is "Mormon and proud of it" he states that "the band don't want me to [talk about it], religion has nothing to do with

The Killers."

Nonetheless, family – if not religion – has to have an indelible effect on someone's personality and, by definition, their star persona. Brandon's older brother Shane was a strong influence, dressing well and looking good. He even went to his Prom with Miss Nevada – setting the bar quite high for his little bro' then, who was over twelve years his junior. It was actually Shane's musical tastes rather than Lotharian good-looks that influenced Brandon most of all. The first time he saw a Smiths video was when Shane showed him; likewise U2's *Rattle & Hum* video ("which was a really big deal because you got to see not only the band but the way the crowd were reacting to them"). The Cars were another favourite of Shane's and by association, Brandon's. In the UK at least, that band will forever be known for 'Drive', the song that sound-tracked Michael Buerke's harrowing news report on Ethiopian famine which in turn prompted a horrified Bob Geldof watching at home to start Band Aid/Live Aid. Yet, aside from this, The Cars were an American rock institution, genuinely gifted and capable of startling moments of emotion. The first cassette album that Brandon bought was by The Cars and for years their frontman, Ric Ocasek, was his favourite star.

Despite only being eight, the Las Vegas 'incomer' to Payson inevitably stood out from the crowd at his school. His musical tastes just reinforced the element of separation from many of his more conservative classmates. One of Brandon's most beloved bands, for example, was Manchester legends The Smiths; Morrissey in particular was something of an icon for him, as he was for millions of people worldwide. Interestingly, Brandon's choice of sports was also unusual. When tracked down by *Hot Press* journalist Stuart Clark to talk about his former school mate [in what is to date the finest article written on the band], The Killers' guitar tech Wyatt Boswell said, "He never had a girlfriend the whole time he lived there. [Nephie, Payson] is a little farm town that thrives on football, so he was seen as a kind of 'off'. 'You play golf? You listen to Elton John?' He caught a lot of shit for that." The Elton John influence extended to fairly rudimentary

Morrissey in particular was something of an icon for him, as he was for millions.

renditions of 'Your Song' and 'The One' on the family piano, interspersed with some sprinklings of Brandon's favourite classical musician, Bach.

Both Shane and Brandon were gifted young golfers and it was this game that was the first draw for the younger brother's voracious ambition. "I don't have time for it at the moment," a by-then-famous Flowers would say in 2005, "but at my best I played to a five-handicap. I was sixteen and thought that maybe I could make it as a pro. I'm glad I didn't because I really don't like those sweaters they wear!"

After six years in Payson, Brandon and his family

returned to Las Vegas where his father found work as a bellman at the Treasure Island Hotel (according to some reports, he was still working this job in the summer of 2005). Brandon was nearly sixteen, with no immediate designs on becoming a pop star.

Ironically, it was his aspirations towards the fairways and manicured greens of the professional golf circuit that coincidentally thrust Brandon towards his first experience of rock and roll. Among the other budding Tiger Woods at the local golf club, he met a fellow golfer who was a huge fan of The Smiths and an unlikely friendship was struck up. As with many teenage friendships which revolve around music, just listening to records soon started to evolve into ideas about making them.

Oddly, given The Smiths' legacy of staggering guitar work courtesy of Johnny Marr, the band they formed – Blush Response – was predominantly a synth-pop outfit. The Pet Shop Boys were a key influence ("I think Neil Tennant's head should be carved on Mount Rushmore," Brandon once said). The Tennant line, "I never thought I would get to be/the creature I was meant to be" is Brandon's favourite lyric of all time. The name is jointly a track from the Vangelis *Blade Runner* album and also, fittingly, a type of make-up.

In what would turn out to be a relatively short and low profile career, Blush Response set about writing songs, rehearsing and listening to as many Eighties albums as they could afford. Meanwhile, across town, Mancunian music was influencing another local musician in a way that would ultimately prove to be crucial to the very existence of The Killers.

CHAPTER 2: THE BRIGHTER SIDE OF LIFE

It is hugely entertaining that the catalyst for The Killers' creation – a band famous for white or mint green suits, a pretty boy singer, and abstinence from the tempting excesses offered by the life of rock – was the Gallagher brothers from Burnage, Manchester, England. Oasis's tempestuous history is well-documented so I won't bore you with it again here, but suffice to say they had arrived on the scene in the mid-Nineties with a slew of classic singles, a fiery sibling relationship/rivalry threatening to implode at any minute and, in Liam Gallagher, a classic frontman. He's famous of course for his aggressive spats with paparazzi, his rock and roll lifestyle, his self-belief/arrogance and celebrity girlfriends/wives. Yet, in a nod to Brandon's own future prowess in interviews,

Liam is actually also one of the masters of the one-liner.

When Oasis made it to Las Vegas as part of some US dates in the late Nineties, most fans were just pleased that the show hadn't been cancelled. Brandon Flowers was there. It was hardly the Sex Pistols at the Manchester Lesser Free Trade Hall, don't get me wrong, but like The Smiths, Buzzcocks, The Fall and Joy Division in the audience at that gig nearly thirty years previous, for the future Killers frontman, it was a show that changed everything.

Brandon had just parted ways with Blush Response. "We were pretty good. I'd come up with vocal melodies and play them on the piano while the girl in the band

When Oasis made it to Las Vegas in the late Nineties, most fans were just pleased that the show hadn't been cancelled.

wrote and sang the lyrics. I never felt right just playing the piano – I was a lead singer trapped in a keyboardist's body, I was living a lie!"

Ultimately, it was a relationship going nowhere, because when the other band members decided to relocate to Los Angeles – a city brutally notorious for chewing up bands, models, actors and entertainers – Brandon did not go. He didn't want to live there and didn't want to pursue a band career there, so he stayed behind in Vegas. He was on his own again, with no band at all. However, his stint in Blush Response had focussed his preference for vocals. Although he does not make it clear whether he is referring to his former band or another unknown outfit when he describes his first efforts on the mike, Brandon reveals that his vocal career was started more out of necessity than of desire. "We demo-ed this one song," he told Austin Scaggs of *Rolling Stone*, "and the singer had the most awful voice I'd ever heard. The guitar player sang it next, and that didn't work. They looked at me. So I went into a little closet, and when I came out the singer obviously didn't like the fact that I was better than him. For them it was hard hitting the notes, but it just came naturally to me. And I loved it."

Anxious to front his own band and fuelled by the guitar-drenched sounds of Oasis, Brandon vowed to start afresh. With more guitars this time. So he did what every self-respecting future pop god does when looking for fellow band members: he looked in the small ads. In among the scattered missives of a thousand no-hopers in the local Vegas weekly was a small box ad searching for musicians into Oasis and Bowie.

That was all it took.

The Killers were born, although they didn't even know it yet.

Dave Keuning wore clogs at school. At least he did when he took part in the annual Tulip Time parade at Pella High. This might sound like the sort of fashion statement that would induce merciless bullying and a Carrie-like mass murder at the Prom, but everyone at the school took part and everyone wore clogs. This was because the city of Pella was formed in the first half of the nineteenth century by The Reverend Hendrik Pieter Scholte, a Dutchman who emigrated from Holland due to the oppressive persecution of the Separatist ideology he and thousands like him followed. While fellow Separatists back at home were often imprisoned by the establishment, Scholte travelled by steamer with his family to the infant north American wilds and settled in Iowa, along with eight hundred fellows of his prospective colony. They quickly purchased 18,000 acres at $1.25 an acre and the foundations of the city of Pella – 'a city of refuge' – were born. The modern-day Pella is a thriving tourist destination, filled with churches, a reputable college and a wealthy business quarter.

This quiet Dutch town bears no resemblance to Las Vegas, the exaggerated modern metropolis that would play such a pivotal role in the birth of The Killers. True, the architecture of Pella was heavily influenced by far-off European shores just like Vegas, although Pella's buildings were rather more sedate and functional than the 'Olde Worlde England' and 'Venice' fashioned by showbiz developers on the Strip and crammed full with one-arm bandits and card tables.

Pella was hardly a city teeming with rock and roll heritage. The kids at future Killers' guitarist Dave's school listened to what many rock-oriented teenagers were checking out in the late Eighties, Aerosmith,

AC/DC and Led Zeppelin. Suitably inspired, Dave bought his first electric guitar aged fourteen. His latterday performances in The Killers seemed a long genealogical leap from these mullet-haired, tight-trousered groups of his childhood, but for now, it was bar chords and bar gigs all the way.

"I just always could hear him practising in his room. We kind of miss that; it's kind of quiet in the house now."

Speaking to Kyle Munson in the *Los Angeles County Register*, Dave's father Chuck was clearly proud of his son's dedication. "He was pretty determined to try and master guitar," said Mr Keuning Senior, now Pella's assistant public works director. "Of course, like most parents, we had no idea he would carry it this far." His mother Sandy added, "I just always could hear him practising in his room. We kind of miss that; it's kind of quiet in the house now."

Back then, the guitar novice Dave quickly improved, such that in his sophomore year he joined the Pella High School Jazz Band. Given the technical prowess and creative bent needed to play competent jazz, this was a good sign for his future songwriting skills. Fortunately, the jazz and classical world did not consume him entirely, as it can so often do with young fledgling musical talents – in 1993 he also joined a Newton-based

Christian rock band called Pickle, with whom he learned much of the basics of being in a gigging band.

Speaking to Munson, Pickles' drummer Keith Nester – now a youth pastor at Christ United Methodist Church in Davenport – was admirably glowing in his recollection of his former band mate. "Dave was just like a monster on guitar at this early age. He was really, really good." Pickles' bassist Kyle Reynolds (who works for appliance maker Maytag Corp) was similarly complimentary: "He always had a real knack for coming up with original riffs and original arrangements to songs."

Given the age-old legacy of 'Before They Were Famous…' celebrity stories in the tabloids once a musician or performer hits the big time, it perhaps reflects very well on Dave's character and personality that his former band mates speak so highly of him. These two former band-mates went on to add that he was shy, quiet, nice and never lost his temper.

Christian music has rarely enjoyed lasting mainstream success, although there are a few notable exceptions: recently Evanescence have sold millions of records and let's not forget (however tempting it may be) Daniel Bedingfield. For his part, Dave's enjoyment of Pickle was mainly for the music and the gigs rather than the religious experience. Also speaking to Munson, he said, "It was cool to be part of something positive. They were great musicians. They helped me get better. They taught me a lot of new things."

Pickle proved to be a great apprenticeship for Dave

and by the time he graduated from Pella High and moved on to Kirkwood Community College (ahead of a place at the University of Iowa), he'd been in Pickle for four years. Unfortunately, his University place "didn't work out" so in 2000 he left and, declining a role within his father's thriving central heating and plumbing business, headed to Las Vegas. His logic was that both New York and Los Angeles were so expensive to live in that they would apply undue financial pressure on him at a time when he needed to be able to take his time

Given the age-old legacy of 'Before They Were Famous…' celebrity stories in the tabloids once a musician or performer hits the big time, it perhaps reflects very well on Dave's character and personality that his former band mates speak so highly of him.

getting his musical ideas and ambitions right. His first stop once in Nevada was to get some money in, so he took a job at a local clothing and shoe store, Banana Republic. Dave knew very few people in Vegas at this point and no musicians.

Within days he was, by his own admission, an expert at folding shirts.

They say the internet makes your life 345,879 times better. Well, not at first for Dave Keuning and Brandon Flowers. Every time Brandon phoned the number from the classifieds advert, the line was engaged. Dave was on t'internet. Fortunately Brandon didn't give up. Brandon never gives up. Eventually, Dave logged off and the phone immediately rang. Words were exchanged and a meeting arranged.

For Dave – who for some reason went by the name of Tavian Go at the time – Brandon's arrival was a Godsend. He'd been laid off from the clothes store job and was unemployed [post-9/11, tourism in Vegas plummeted, as it did globally]; he used this enforced sabbatical to write and write and write, becoming a prolific songwriter during what otherwise would have been a very depressing period.

His own original material aside, however, he still needed to find a band. When the auditions started, he sat with a litany of "freaks" who had replied to his advert. One was cross-eyed and another was inked with tattoos listing how many dead people he had in his immediate family. When Brandon appeared, he looked "normal", although Dave has pointed out when they first met he was wearing Hush Puppies ("because Oasis did"). For me, that would have finished it there and then, but Dave is made of sterner stuff, because that particular lightweight choice of footwear was taken as an indicator of common ground. Perhaps he'd spent too many hours extolling the virtues of the stock in Banana Republic but, whatever the reason, the Hush Puppies were enough to make Dave sit up and take notice. Hardly a safety-pin through the nose, I know, but each to their own.

Shortly after this initial meet, Brandon went over to Dave's house, his keyboard tucked under his arm [it wasn't covered in spangly rhinestones at this point]. That very afternoon they started fiddling around with song ideas and, incredibly given the track's impact on The Killers' future career, the genesis of 'Mr Brightside' was begun. Dave had a verse, Brandon wrote the chorus soon after and that was that. This immediate creative chemistry parallels the famous Morrissey and Marr partnership that produced so many Smiths classics.

At the time of writing, The Killers have played 'Mr Brightside' at every single gig they've ever performed. If they ever split up only to reform twenty years later for a nostalgia tour, no doubt playing in the very same lizard lounges that Vegas thrives on, it will be this very song that the cigar-smoking crowd will be listening out for.

It was the first song they ever wrote.

Even as early as this, Dave looks back and hints that he thought there was a unique atmosphere already. "When I first met Brandon, he just came in and threw out some song ideas that he had and I really knew that they were something special ... That was always my motivation, so I could keep writing and keep working on this music, I don't want to sound conceited, but I thought we had a good chance."

The Killers' line-up that we know so well was a little way off yet, however. The first Killers drummer and bassist were an eighteen-year-old sticksman known as

THE KILLERS

Dell Star and a bassist said to be in his thirties by the rather fantastic name of Buss Bradley. There is little known about either of these early members, who were working in the band around the summer of 2002.

Prior to these latter events, this early line-up clearly did make a start though, as several interviews exist, albeit mainly with *Las Vegas Weekly*, where Dave is referred to only as Tavian Go. In these interviews The Killers talk of wanting to make "a full-length CD" and setting up a debut tour as soon as possible.

CHAPTER 3: THE KILLERS CRYSTALLISE

Mark Stoermer is six-foot five-inches tall. He sports a digital watch made of plastic that was so beloved of anyone who owned a ZX Spectrum (32K, not just 16K, check out the power) and played *Dungeons & Dragons*, back when shoulder pads were wide and Thatcher was in the middle of ruining Britain. He had designs on becoming "a lawyer or college professor or something academic" but, due to the success of The Killers these dreams currently remain unfulfilled. Instead of spending years hidden away in some crusty library giving seminars to pupils who don't care about subjects that don't matter and all the while earning a pittance, Mark would have to get used to earning millions of dollars, being adored by fans all over the world and living the life of a globally feted pop star. As George Best once said when he was asked about being rich, famous and married to Miss World, *where did it all go wrong?*

Prior to The Killers' success, Mark was a medical courier which, according to various reports, involved biking countless grotesque body parts around for a local laboratory. One magazine even suggested he spent most of his working hours couriering boxers' urine samples.

He dabbled early on with the trumpet – his father was in a big band – but soon became obsessed with the guitar and then bass. Learning on a six-string has undoubtedly given his bass lines a distinctive degree of melody that might be lacking in a player who had never ventured outside of four strings. By his own admission, he came to most styles of music fairly late on, apparently never having listened to rock until he heard Nirvana. The benefit of the courier job was that he could spend all day with headphones on riding around Vegas listening to a glut of varied music: Rolling Stones, U2, New Order, Jimi Hendrix, The Who, Macca and so on. The McCartney influence is interesting, as listeners to The Killers' debut album will note Mark's extensive use of a pick, an unpopular mode of playing for most rock bassists, but one that nevertheless gives his lines a very powerful, clean punch. He has also said he is specifically a fan of Hendrix's bassist Noel Redding and, of course, the inimitable nimble-fingered late John Entwistle of The Who, whose four line solo in 'My Generation' probably remains the single most identifiable bass solo in modern rock.

Mark played bass constantly, picking up ideas from people like Duran Duran's under-rated (yes, I did say that) John Taylor. He delved even further back than that. "Roxy Music were the predecessors to Duran Duran and all those kind of groups. They have influenced me specifically in The Killers. I take a little bit from their bass lines." Oddly, perhaps, Mark was also heavily into prog rockers Pink Floyd: "Roger Waters is one of my favourite bassists and inspired me to play."

The Killers' frontman Brandon Flowers is the only member of the band born in Las Vegas. Guitarist Dave Keuning was born in Des Moines, Iowa; Mark was only brought up there and the final piece of the jigsaw, one Ronnie Vannucci, was also only brought up there. Perhaps it would be fair to say, when compared to his future band-mates, Ronnie was a more conventional US kid. He was good at sports and his musical tastes were consistent with the popular choices of the day. Unusually qualified for a drummer, Ronnie studied percussion to degree level at the University of Nevada-Las Vegas (UNLV) on his classical music course, immediately putting him in a different bracket to about 99.9% of rock drummers. His tastes in music reinforced this idea that he was not your average drummer. Tom Waits was "the man for me" he later said, "dusty, romantic, dark songwriting." He was also a fan of Tom Petty, about whom he said, "[his] 'American Girl' "reminds me of travelling with my dad in his old ford F1-50 when I was little." Ronnie's father was actually a competent guitar player with a good ear for music and he has said this undoubtedly helped him start his career when he was very young.

Ronnie was a relatively experienced musician and boasted stints in various pre-Killers bands such as rocksteady outfit Attaboy Skip. Old friend PJ Perez saw this band several times: "[They] sounded a lot like The Mighty Mighty Bosstones," he reveals. "I worked with one of their sax players, and actually approached Ronnie to come and drum with me, but he was already juggling two or three other things and couldn't." The band's set was an eclectic mix of ska, metal and pop, including a cover version of Twisted Sister's 'We're Not Gonna Take It' and the Ghostbusters theme tune.

At the time he first met Brandon and Dave, Ronnie

Mark and Ronnie – who were regular, known faces on the Vegas gig circuit – were approached about possibly joining the band. They said yes and in the process changed all four of their lives forever.

was a photographer at the Little Chapel of Flowers in Las Vegas. Not for long. With the original line-up of The Killers not working out, Mark and Ronnie – who were regular, known faces on the Vegas gig circuit – were approached about possibly joining the band. They said yes and in the process changed all four of their lives forever.

Chronologically, it appears that Mark was the last piece of the jigsaw to fall into place in Sept 2002, as an interview in the *Las Vegas Weekly* describes the band as "like no other noise in the city of lounge acts and cover bands, The Killers ... prove that there is hope for a music scene that is oft-criticized for lacking originality and stamina ... The only ingredient missing in this near-perfect rock-band equation is a bass player, whom they are seeking."

Like his former contemporaries in Pickle, Dave immediately impressed Ronnie, despite the latter's far more impressive technical qualifications: "He's one of the most talented musicians I've come across. He has extremely good cars, a good sense of melody." And melody, my friends, is what The Killers are all about.

The Killers were not the first Killers. In the New Order video for their track 'Crystal', a fictional band of that name are featured, complete with 'The Killers' emblazoned on the bass drum. Brandon's group saw the video, liked the name and christened themselves as the non-fictional version. They liked the fact the fictional band was supposed to be the perfect combination of youth, looks and talent, it was something to aspire to. Confusingly, Brandon also later pointed out that "part of the reason we picked the name The Killers is it's a contradiction. I remember reading about T Rex and seeing how Marc Bolan was such a little guy."

But it was the New Order connection that was the key.

As a huge fan, Brandon would later see a dream come true in the summer of 2005 at T In The Park festival when New Order invited him on stage to join them in a rendition of 'Crystal': "That was amazing, I'd never even seen a full set of theirs before, so that was perfect for me."

The combination of Brandon's youthful confidence and the other three's more experienced approach would quickly reveal itself to be a potent force. Early rehearsals were in a garage with no windows and a room temperature just below that of the surface of the sun, given Nevada's climate and the proximity of the 'fiery hell on earth' that is nearby Death Valley. One afternoon the sweating band did a temperature check which read 120 degrees.

When the garage wasn't available (presumably it was pre-booked by a lawnmower or strimmer), The Killers' own website biog explains they would use the facilities at Ronnie's University, a full 2000 square feet of state-of-the-art rehearsal space provided by the Uni for their would-be classical virtuosos. They shipped in their own guitar amps (also used for Brandon's vocals), their own bass and keyboard, and Ronnie nestled in behind a kit supposed to be for the "UNLV pep drum band".

The first ever 'Killers' gig was at the Café Roma in Dave and Brandon's home-town and actually pre-dates the first shows by the line-up that eventually gelled permanently. Prior to the other future members joining, the duo played 'Mr Brightside' and 'Replaceable' at an open-mike night at this tiny venue across from UNLV.

"[It was] a hip little place," Brandon told Austin Scaggs of *Rolling Stone*, "where kids in black Converses could go drink coffee and smoke … It was terrible, awful. Before we went on, I was looking for a place on the floor to get rid of whatever I'd eaten that day. I didn't throw up, but after my voice broke a couple of times I decided that I'd just play keyboards, because singing made me so nervous."

"Before we went on, I was looking for a place on the floor to get rid of whatever I'd eaten that day. I didn't throw up, but after my voice broke a couple of times I decided that I'd just play keyboards, because singing made me so nervous."

Following this inauspicious start and with the more familiar line-up now realised, The Killers would still struggle to get frequent shows. The problem for any aspiring band in Las Vegas is that if they are not after 'regular work' playing lounges and casinos, the city's past and present musical achievements are not encouraging. Flicking through the *Who's Who* of Vegas rock and roll is not exactly like a trip to the Music Hall of Fame. It's a city that allows Celine Dion to perform there nightly for years on end, for a start, but she's an outsider so that doesn't count. Wayne Newton is a native and has played in excess of 25,000 concerts in the city over forty years. But he's unlikely to make the front cover of *NME*. The list of famous 'alternative' (as in alternative to Celine Dion, Elton John et al) bands who have sprung up from there is as long as, well, a very short arm: Slaughter, Crystal Method, Curl Up and Die … that's about it. Metal, hardcore, lounge music, and The Killers.

When The Killers were first starting to develop, the main alternative strain of music in the city was metal,

"It was hard at first 'cause no one knew who we were. We were playing with other metal bands and their audience just didn't know what to think of us."

usually aggressive, leather-edged, long-haired and soundtracked by crunching guitars.

The Killers were none of the above.

Consequently, local gigs were hard to come by. When they did book a show, it was often supporting the (then) more-popular metal and punk bands in front of their testosterone-filled audiences. "It was hard at first 'cause no one knew who we were. We were playing with other metal bands and their audience just didn't know what to think of us," recalls Dave.

Fortunately, as Ronnie told *Chik* magazine, they found one pivotal outlet that was typically showbiz, a transvestite bar called Sascha's (it later changed its name to Tramps and then Trans). "Our friend Ryan – who is actually our merchandising guy now – was doing these DJ shows at a couple of different nightclubs and he landed this one … it was just a cool hangout, and Ryan would bring in different DJs, as well as DJ himself. Then he started bringing in a band and we started playing there about once a month. We would always have a really good turnout and a good time. We always got funny looks at first, because we're a Vegas band and Vegas bands aren't very good – they're a bit behind."

The bar served food and drinks so there was always going to be a hint of cabaret about the gigs. There were clusters of couches and some people would sit there for hours hanging out, next to bums who were happy just to have somewhere comfortable to sit until they were thrown out at six the next morning.

But at least The Killers were able to perform in front of a crowd regularly which is more than most of their Vegas contemporaries were able to do. Their regular slot was every Sunday for the Eighties theme night. Without the benefit of hindsight, if this was the highlight of The Killers' gigging week, it might have been easy for them to have concurred with the slogan, "Vegas is the last destination for recording artists rather than the springboard for new ones."

When *Hot Press* magazine's Stuart Clark tracked down an old musician friend of Ronnie's by the name of PJ Perez, it was interesting to note that prior to flying to England for their debut shows there, The Killers' profile was really very limited back in Vegas. Perez talks of them playing "dive bars, English pubs, video poker bars" as well as the aforementioned drag bar. "They were always going on last after all the other bands who didn't sound anything like them had played, so the crowds weren't the greatest," recalls Perez. "More often than not though, they'd win whoever was there and get asked back. Their biggest Vegas show would have been the farewell one they did at Tramps to two or three hundred people."

One review by Jarret Keene in the *Las Vegas Press* from their last show at Tramps suggested the band were already improving at such a rate that big things were around the corner: "Christ, this band has come a long way from their sorry-ass performances around this time last year. Now the band plays the tightest, slickest, most vicious set of pop tunes I've heard in Las Vegas in the two ho-hum years I've covered this scene. Somebody is grooming these guys for the big leagues, and the effort has clearly paid off. Most of the old, crappy numbers are gone, replaced by unhappy, shiny, infinitely superior ones."

CHAPTER 4: SUCH A JEALOUS GUY

Like a holiday romance without the contraception, The Killers were born of an affair between their very American roots and the absurdly Anglo-centric sounds of Britpop and countless other UK bands. You could say Britpop – or perhaps more accurately, British music in general – was their absent father. There for their creation but thousands of miles away for their day-to-day development.

One rumoured but unlikely influence on The Killers' sound is alleged to be the little-known UK punk-thrash outfit The Chocolate Speedway Riders. This cult band were so 'cult' they never signed a record deal, never took on a manger or agent and passed into oblivion after a twenty-three month career. They were a musical anomaly at the turn of the Nineties when grunge was the *modus operandi* for any aspiring band.

America's western seaboard underground circuit had given us Nirvana, Pearl Jam, *Nevermind*, Soundgarden, Courtney Love, 'slacker culture', Sub Pop and a generation of 'loser' fans. 'Grunge', so-called in an early article on the scene by Everett True, transformed modern music, fashion, radio programming, music TV, the gig circuit and pretty much every element of the rock and roll world. Of course, in a few short years, grunge would in turn be slayed by Britpop, a self-professed antidote to all things American and the purveyor of cheeky British pop, Oasis, Blur, Pulp, Supergrass, Fred Perry shirts, greyhounds and, er, Shed Seven.

But back in 1991, The Chocolate Speedway Riders had started the rot. Grunge, MTV and all that jazz meant nothing to them. They played thrash punk, barely listenable to most ears. It made Nirvana's 'Territorial Pissings' sound like the *Andy Pandy* theme tune. Their lyrics were absurd, and titles like 'What The Fucking Hell Does Dennis Norden Actually Do?' and 'Syphilis On My Upper Lip' (a crowd favourite) meant their commercial career was doomed to be at best minimal. Live shows were frantic, an entire set of eleven songs being delivered in an aurally-exhausting 25 minutes. Fringes were long, boots were thick and filthy, the crowds tiny. Legend has it that their final show was attended only by a brother of the bassist, who thought it was "shit".

But what the Choccies had that made them different – back then at least – was Stefano on keyboards. Not your typical thrash-punk band member's name but there you go. He played keyboards loud and most importantly of all, usually through a guitar distortion pedal. He abhorred grunge and worshipped Eighties synth-pop outfits like Depeche Mode, Yazoo and The Cure. But his band played punk thrash. So that was what he played. At the time keyboards were about as popular as a loose bullet on the International Space Station, but with a name like Stefano, he was used to being unpopular.

The point here is this – listening to the crackly mp3 files posted on the not-updated-since-1996 Choccies website ("we've got better things to do"), you can hear keyboard fills and chord sequences that remind one immediately of The Killers. This might be urban myth – all attempts at tracking down the Choccies met with one dead end after another – but the sound is definitely there. Maybe The Killers have never heard the Chocolate Speedway Riders – few people did – but it is hard not to be reminded of them when listening to The Killers.

One better-known and less unhealthy influence is obviously Depeche Mode; The Killers themselves hail The Cure as a key band they look to; Duran Duran, Pet Shop Boys, OMD are all musically somewhere in The Killers' family tree. Countless pages of magazines have been used up discussing the influences on the band, but the main point is this: The Killers take all these myriad influences, push them through their own songwriting blender and make the end-product something decidedly unique, modern and frankly greater than the sum of its parts.

The Killers hooked up with their manager early on and in a very interesting way. They had posted some songs on-line at lasvegasmusicscene.com, a local site that people could check out new bands and songs. He was browsing around the web looking for interesting stuff when he saw the name The Killers, listened to the files, liked them and that was that.

The ease with which The Killers initially got a US record deal was in stark contrast to how quickly they met their manager. Put simply, at first no one was interested, at least not enough to actually sign them. Wisely as it turned out, the band and manager decided to fly over to the UK for some small shows and test the water out over that side of the pond. What a decision that was.

Enter Lizard King.

The Killers' second ever show outside Las Vegas was actually at Camden's Dublin Castle in September of 2003. So green were they around the gills that some of the band had to apply for a passport in order to travel at all (the urban myth that only 7% of Americans have passports seems to extend to rock stars).

To their eternal credit, it was the UK's independent label Lizard King who were the first record label to take a risk with The Killers. It might not seem like much of a risk given the debut album's omnipresence in the charts and favour with critics, but all this success and profile was very much after the fact. When Lizard King first heard The Killers' demo, it appears there was no hype or competition for their signatures.

Lizard King was only set up in 2003 by former President of Arista UK, Martin Heath and a finance expert, Dominic Hardisty. On the team were Siona Ryan and Ben Durling, the latter of whom was the A&R man who would capture the band's signatures on contracts. Siona was heavily involved too, meeting the band when they came over that very first time to the UK to play

"The gig was mainly industry heads who were there, including quite a few A&R people who weren't sure if they were signed or not."

shows at a host of 'toilet' venues on the pub circuit. As Siona told *Hot Press's* Stuart Clark, when they played the Camden Barfly, "being so early it was mainly industry heads who were there, including quite a few A&R people who weren't sure if they were signed or not."

They weren't signed, but not for long. Durling heard the forthcoming album's two strongest tracks, 'Mr Brightside' and 'Somebody Told Me' and to him it was an easy decision to make. "I thought it was a pretty obvious thing at the time. The whole Eighties revival was starting to rear its head in the UK and The Killers were potentially a perfect fit. Bands like The Strokes and The White Stripes had also made it cool to be American again, so the timing felt really right."

So convinced were Lizard King of the band's potential that when they signed them they still hadn't heard all of the debut album, only five actual completed songs. The point was, they'd heard enough.

Although in retrospect The Killers seemed very focussed in the way they conquered the UK first, in reality Dave says it was not quite so pre-meditated: "It wasn't like a genius plot to rule the world or anything.

One of the great opening rock riffs of all time, no question. But The Killers don't stop there. There are hooks all over the place ... vocal catches, bass twists and keyboard lines.

It was more like America didn't like us at first. They kinda rejected us. We tried to play and get signed and all that. We played a few other cities. But in England, it's almost like they like new music more, and we got signed to an indie label in the UK because that's all that was offered."

The Killers signed to Lizard King in July of 2003 and even as early as that, songs such as 'Mr Brightside' were getting regular airings on BBC Radio 1, notably Zane Lowe's *Evening Session*; veteran Steve Lamacq was also a big fan.

Zane Lowe was particularly impressed with the song

that The Killers and Lizard King put out as their debut single as a limited edition of only a few hundred copies in September 2003. It was their oldest song, the one that Dave and Brandon had written when they hooked up at that very first rehearsal together. It was called 'Mr Brightside'. It was the song that changed everything for The Killers.

You've all heard it by now. It was probably the first time you heard or saw anything from Mssr Flowers and Co. And what a single it was. The opening riff is like an intravenous hit, it has the ability to immediately pick you up, no matter where you hear it and when. Almost two years later, when The Killers played a soaking wet Glastonbury 2005 in front of 100,000 people, as the time came to play this song Dave was standing cool as you like, one foot on his monitor. When he picked out the arpeggio-like riff, it *instantly* sent tens of thousands of people ballistic. One of the great opening rock riffs of all time, no question.

But The Killers don't stop there. There are hooks all over the place, vocal catches, bass twists and keyboard lines after each chorus that you just can't get out of your head. Take, for example, the ascending and descending, treated keyboard chords that push the song on to its climax right around the final vocal restraints. You think the song can't gather any more momentum, can't lift you any higher and then they hit you with a chord sequence that is very Eighties yet at the same time could be some kind of pseudo-classical movement. This is songwriting of the highest order.

Brandon carries the lyrics, his sick lullaby, rammed with gut-wrenching jealousy and anxiety about his unfaithful girlfriend, with consummate ease. There is genuine raw emotion in his voice, perhaps because the subject matter is, by his own admission, very much a real-life experience. The sporadic use of double-layered vocals is crafty, implying that the jealousy which eats Mr Brightside up is almost like a demonic inner voice, Beezlebub on his shoulder. Contrast this with the second verse's sparse vocal line where Brandon is singing alone, the band have dropped out of the mix, and Brightside is suddenly and painfully alone, by himself, betrayed. It's a masterpiece. Some observers have said 'Mr Brightside' is an iconic post-Millennial pop classic and I don't think that is mere hyperbole.

Ronnie later told reporters that Brandon could possibly be Mr Brightside. Although Brandon himself has never said he is Mr Brightside, he did tell *Q* magazine about one experience with a former girlfriend that Mr B could have related to – having suspected she was seeing someone else, he went into an English pub (what else?) one night and saw her with him: "I guess I should have done something but I'm not a violent person. But it really affected me. I would physically throw up ... jealousy is a terrible, terrible experience."

As Julia Roberts' character said in *Pretty Woman*, "big mistake, *huge*." "I wouldn't be here if we hadn't written Mr Brightside. I have no regrets. And they've split up now, so I hear. She knows she fucked up."

It's hard to imagine now, but when 'Mr Brightside'

was first released, The Killers were an unknown band and their single was just another CD sitting on a thousand desks in a pile with a thousand other singles. Not surprisingly, *NME* was one of the first UK mags to review the single: "If you will, the flipside to The Strokes," they suggested. "'Mr Brightside' sounds as massive and magnificent as impossibly filthy, drugged-up sex with strangers. Ambition, sex, noise; no filler, these Killers." Writer Toby L was equally smitten: "The Killers' debut is a scintillating marriage of ascending

"Where their demo tracks were muddled, hodgepodge affairs, their debut single is brimming with confidence and character."

and flittering guitars, entwined with choral-elevation … it's ringing in your own ears for a reason; *succumb*. A potentially glorious future awaits – as do we, with open arms."

The Las Vegas Mercury was quick to point out the vast evolution from previous recordings: "Where their demo tracks were muddled, hodgepodge affairs, exploring a variety of influences but never settling on a signature sound, their debut single is brimming with confidence and character."

Impressively so early on in their career, the 'quality' British newspapers were behind them. Take this review from *The Times*: "Once in a blue moon such a debut single arrives. The old shiver up the spine is present for sure ... three minutes and 41 seconds of synth-pop perfection."

Shortly after in November, *NME* put out a cover mount CD with 'Jenny Was A Friend Of Mine' included, which for many UK fans was the first time they would have actually had chance to play a Killers track. For Brandon, the coverage in the mag must have been exciting as being such a fan of UK music it was something of a bible to him growing up. "*NME* has always been a big deal in my house because my older brother always had it pinned up to the wall," he later told reporters.

The single and these early UK dates were mixed with more isolated shows in the US, such as acoustic sessions for influential DJ Matt Pinfield and also an appearance at the industry-mobbed CMJ Music Festival in New York in October, 2003. Still unsigned in the US at this point, it was after CMJ that their management's office was besieged with calls from major labels. Finally, The Killers signed with Island Def Jam.

At one fantastic Detroit show, they supported the seminal Dirtbombs – a band which preceded The White Stripes and is revered by most of the American music biz – and were watched, oddly enough, by 'Bridget Jones', aka Renee Zellwegger, who was a close friend of The White Stripes' lead singer, Jack White.

Inevitably with such interest, more UK live dates were scheduled and the series of shows in late 2003 complemented the growing fascination with the band. With British Sea Power also playing at most shows, The

Killers ploughed through scores of dates – albeit at very small venues at this stage – during the autumn and winter of 2003 in the UK. The show at Camden's Barfly venue saw several hundred fans left outside unable to get a ticket while inside key journalists and record business personnel were in abundance.

"Tonight simply breaks the mould; finally, the British music-insiders have succumbed, and now it's your turn."

Samantha Hall was one of the lucky few who crammed into this very early Killers show at The Barfly and she made no secret of her feelings in a review for the excellent homereviewsconcerts.com website: "Beating out fat, obese tune after fat, glitzy tune, their hometown Vegas glamour dribbles all over the miniscule stage. Reactions are riotous – whoops and cries of 'encore' are rare – about as rare as you *not* thinking of Elvis when we mention a Vegas rock band. Yet not on this occasion. Tonight simply breaks the mould; jiggling industry types are abound – for once, some smiling, others clapping – the supposed 'cool observers' at the back ... Finally, the British music-insiders have succumbed, and now it's your turn."

After the UK autumn dates, The Killers were very nearly, er, killed when they flew home to Las Vegas and caught a connecting flight to Houston, Texas. Their plane hit an air pocket and entered free-fall, plummeting several thousand feet before managing to stabilise itself. Such events seem to follow them around: when they were recording some album tracks, they had to travel through bush fires in the Simi Valley to get to the studio and during the recording of 'Believe Me, Natalie' the studio was hit by a minor earthquake which actually shook Ronnie from his drum stool.

It was a heady time. Later observations would imply that The Killers had neatly plugged into the vogue among US music biz circles for late Seventies-early Eighties disco-punk retro-ism, but this is complete nonsense, given that until Lizard King took a punt on them in the UK, no one in their homeland seemed at all interested (some reports have Warners declining them, although it is unclear if this was before or after Lizard King). Already they were being interviewed by the UK broadsheets as the biggest new band of the year – "we can go to Sheffield and play to more people than we can in Vegas," as Brandon so succinctly put it. So, this was not a case of Ramones versus Pistols, New York versus London, US versus UK, Vegas versus, er, Blackpool, there was no chicken and egg mystery to who discovered The Killers first. It was the UK.

CHAPTER 5: GIGS AND THE TOP TEN

With the backing of two labels, one major, one indie, The Killers were put into the studio in late 2003 to record their debut album, to be titled *Hot Fuss*. Veteran mixer Alan Moulder was on board for the sessions at Eden Studios in Chiswick in early December 2003. Having formerly worked with Depeche Mode, the Smashing Pumpkins and – not worthy, not worthy – The Smiths, The Killers knew that they were moving in lofty circles indeed. Oddly, it was Moulder's work on hardcore industrialists Nine Inch Nails' *The Fragile* that convinced The Killers to bring him to help with the album's creation. Further work was done in the San Fernando Valley, Chatsworth and also more mixing with

Mark Needham who had famously worked with Fleetwood Mac.

A revealing conversation with Nicole Roberge in *Soundwaves* magazine shed some light into the band's fairly fluid attitude to writing new material: "I don't put too much thought into [worrying about writing], it takes the fun out of it. If it's a good song, it's a good song," explained Brandon. "A lot of people pick things apart, but if it's catchy, that's a great thing. And if the lyrics are great, then that's even better. There's people that worry and want to know exactly where the bass should be in the mix and if the drums are lined up and if that all technically sounds great. No, it's, 'does it sound good or doesn't it?' The other stuff doesn't matter."

Although sessions were wrapped up before Christmas, the actual final master copy wasn't completed at the lab until mid-February 2004 [mastered by Brian "Big Bass" Gardner (Blink-182, Eminem)] by which time the anticipation and demand for a Killers' album was frenetic.

As one year turned into another, it was hoped 2004 would be an eventful twelve months. Ideally, the band hoped their debut album would sell a healthy amount, possibly 50,000 maybe even 100,000 copies worldwide. Tours might sell well and press coverage would remain strong. Yeah, right! The band should have known this would all soon seem like small fry when *NME* named them as one of the Top Ten bands to watch in 2004 [America's *Rolling Stone* would only agree they were 'one to watch' eight months later]. In fact, as events transpired, The Killers were *the* band to watch in 2004

... by a country mile.

Yet more UK dates were played in February 2004 with the up-and-coming Stellastar*; then more shows back in the US mid-March including two gigs in one day at the South-by Southwest convention; then it was back on the road with Stellastar* for scores of American gigs as well as a handful of solo headline slots, then to cap off a hectic spell with barely a day off at all, they played the Coachella Festival on May 1.

It seemed like quite a gap between the seismic impact of 'Mr Brightside' as the debut single and the follow-up,

Ideally, the band hoped their debut album would sell a healthy amount, possibly 50,000 maybe even 100,000 copies worldwide. Tours might sell well and press coverage would remain strong.

the equally brilliant 'Somebody Told Me', which wasn't released until early March, 2004. The single was pre-empted by that rash of yet more UK shows with Stellastar* as main support. After the show at the prestigious ICA, Mark performed a two-hour DJ set under the pseudonym of DJ Perfect Storm at Camden's Barfly. By the time the song was actually available in the shops, Radio 1 was reported to be playing it over thirty five times a week. Zane Lowe welcomed the band in to his studio for a three-song session to further increase the momentum.

The single was backed with 'The Ballad of Michael Valentine' and 'Under The Gun' and, in suitably Eighties fashion, was also released as a 7" pink vinyl single only backed with 'The Ballad of Michael Valentine'. Boy George would be proud. The first two hundred copies came with a poster and were signed by

These dates ideally primed the UK ... by the time they came to play London in that summer month, demand was so vast that three shows had to be booked in the capital, all of which easily sold out.

the band. Later, a remix by Josh Harris was available by download. At the time, 'Somebody Told Me' reached only Number 28 in the charts, but sold close to 10,000 copies. [This track would ultimately be re-released many months later like its predecessor, more of which later.]

Not wishing to miss too many days without a gig, the relentless march of The Killers continued with a twenty five-date tour of the US in April, starting in Portland and ending in Phoenix Arizona. Again Stellastar* were the main support band. With barely a pause for breath, the band hopped back on a plane and bounced across the

Atlantic once again for the planned re-release of 'Mr Brightside' in May. As was now expected, this came with a batch of yet more live shows, their first proper headline tour of the UK (where the single was also re-released in May 2004, reaching Number 3). These dates ideally primed the UK for the forthcoming debut album release, in the first week of June. By the time they came to play London in that summer month, demand was so vast that three shows had to be booked in the capital, all of which easily sold out.

This time around, 'Mr Brightside' [b/w 'Change your Mind'] was B-listed at Radio 1, and most commercial stations with any interest in chart music found a strong placing for it on their playlists too. By now, there were few new music fans in the UK who weren't aware of the band and this interest was backed up by a much broader section of music TV channels taking the re-shot promo clip for the single (filmed at Staten Island only a few weeks earlier). In keeping with their penchant for coloured vinyl, the single was also available in two other formats: firstly, b/w 'Somebody Told Me' (Insider Remix)/'Midnight Show' and including the actual video; secondly, there was another 7" vinyl, this time in bright red with a gatefold sleeve *a la* any Seventies prog rock and heavy metal band, where the lead track was backed by 'Who Let You Go?'.

Whereas the first release of the single was 'excluded' from the chart listing largely due to the limited numbers available, this time around the song entered the listings at Number 10, an amazing achievement. The actual sales for the song would later nearly be doubled by those of the early 2005 single 'Somebody Told Me', but between now and then The Killers would become one of the biggest bands in the world.

Their first Top Ten placing saw them right up there with classics such as 'Fuck It' by Eamon, and its 'reply' song by Frankee, so beautifully-titled 'Fuck You Right Back'. Despite the latter being Number 1 (as Toyah once

For now, they were in the UK Top Ten, home to all their music heroes. Home to The Cure, Depeche Mode, OMD, Oasis, David Bowie et al.

said, "it's a myshteree"), the actual Top Ten the last week in May was a mighty fine one. Aside from these two gimmick songs, The Killers were keeping good company with the likes of Kelis ('Trick Me'), 411 Featuring Ghostface Killah ('On My Knees' – oh, the chaffing), the under-rated Kristian Leontiou ('Story Of My Life') and the excellent and recently cancer-free Anastacia ('Left Outside Alone').

For now, they were in the UK Top Ten, home to all their music heroes. Home to Elvis, The Beatles, the Stones, The Who and, more pertinently, The Cure, Depeche Mode, OMD, Oasis, David Bowie et al. The issue was, after such a swift rise to prominence, could The Killers make it a more permanent arrangement?

"I'm actually pretty aloof when it comes to the lyrics. I don't write them. I just listen to the music. I never pay attention to the lyrics, so your average fan would probably know better than I would."
Dave Keuning

During this swathe of live dates, one of the rumours that began sweeping around Killers' fans websites – followers of the band call themselves 'Victims' – was that they were planning to film a 'murder mystery trilogy'. When I heard this I thought of hotels in the country and conference rooms being used by David Brent-style managers to 'bond' their team. Fortunately, The Killers had other ideas.

Showing an unusual degree of depth and creativity, The Killers have indeed mooted the idea of a 25-minute long-form film/video almost since they first appeared on rock's front pages. The idea, so they told us, was to film

Rumours began sweeping around Killers' fans websites – followers of the band call themselves 'Victims' – that they were planning to film a 'murder mystery trilogy'.

The Murder Trilogy based around three of their songs: 'Midnight Show', 'Jenny Was A Friend Of Mine' and the as-yet-unreleased and heard-by-only-a-few 'Leave

The Bourbon On The Shelf'. The final track is the most mythologised of all The Killers back-catalogue – played at their very early shows and heard by only a lucky few, the track became the song equivalent of an early Sex Pistols gig, with thousands claiming to have heard it but literally only a few hundred actually having done so (real fans, real 'Victims' know it by the MI5-style abbreviation 'LTBOTS'). It's a vg kool trak, btw. Cue more press and hype, courtesy of The Killers.

The narrative thread of the trilogy centres around a relationship that began full of hope ('LTBOTS') but has sadly gone wrong. Instead of parting ways and slagging each other off over a pint with mates, the boy kills the girl and gets rid of the body ('MS') and then denies all knowledge of said grisly act ('JWAFOM'). Brandon gave scant detail of the actual storyline, proferring little more than an evasive "there was water involved, although he didn't drown her". Filming at Las Vegas' Lake Mead has been suggested for some of the scenes.

Of course, they were by far not the first band to dabble in celluloid, but this had a twist – in more ways than one – that made the proposed project very intriguing. Bands often put out material or releases in between albums to keep momentum running fast and ensure that in the chew-em-up-spit-em-out culture of the modern music biz, those beloved but oh-so-fickle fans don't forget them too soon. So the prospect of a film was an exciting one for all concerned. Nonetheless, details remained sketchy throughout much of 2005 with little more than a repeated mention of the actor James Spader as the possible killer surfacing in the press.

'Mr Brightside' was released in America much later than its original UK date, and as mentioned the band shot a fresh video for that territory which reinforced the connections with New Order. The director for the shoot, one Sophie Muller, was the very same woman who had shot the promo clip for 'Crystal' from which The Killers took their name. Muller was also responsible for amazing videos for bands such as Blur, Coldplay and No Doubt so the band had a great time working with her for two days in the scorching heat of the San Fernando Valley near Los Angeles for the new clip.

By the time they were working with Sophie, it was the band's fourth video shoot and easily their biggest production to date. Filming was in an old warehouse that was rumoured to have been used for several porn films in the past (*The Fillers* maybe?). The set was very extravagant, akin to something out of *Moulin Rouge*, and the beautiful leading lady fitted perfectly, a Polish actress and dancer by the name of Isabella Miko who was better known as one of the lead characters in the box office hit movie *Coyote Ugly*. The atmosphere of Wild West mixed with Moulin Rouge was seen at its best in the characterful and intimidating features of the bordello owner, Eric Roberts, brother of Julia. With the video finding favour on most music channels and the song enjoying a renewed profile, The Killers found themselves with one of 2005's most popular karaoke anthems in the thousands of bars in New York.

THE KILLERS

Yet even iconic karaoke status had to take a back seat to the release of The Killers' debut album, *Hot Fuss*, in June 2004.

From whence it all came: Las Vegas, gamblers' paradise, casinos, all-you-can-eat buffets, showgirls ... and The Killers.

Despite their pin-up image, The Killers' success is heavily fuelled by relentless gigging, week after week, after week.

"I knew I shouldn't have put these trousers in on 60."
Brandon Flowers strikes out once more for men in tight pants.

Dave Keuning in pristine white – somehow managing to look like
a Seventies throw-back and yet super-cool at the same time.

Ronnie Vannucci: aside from Bonham and Moon,
the most entertaining drummer in rock.

Mark Stoerming, sideburns bristling, a supreme bassist.

Perhaps not Brandon's number one fans: The Bravery.

Something The Killers are getting used to: picking up yet another gong at the World Music Awards, August, 2005.

Touring can be incredibly boring – The Killers
play Twister for the cameras.

Live 8, July 2005. Now that's what you call a picnic in the park.

The Killers come full circle – on stage with
New Order at T In The Park, 2005.

Signing autographs for a new generation of fans
at the filming of *The OC*.

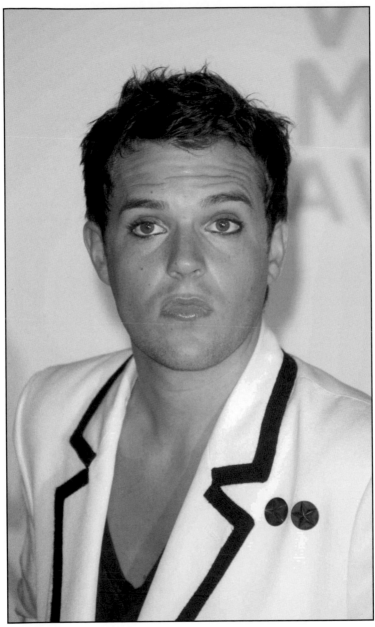

"Great music is great music, but image is priceless. I'm not saying I'm in this position because I'm good looking, but it certainly helps."

A synth-pop-rock band with the keyboard player on lead vocal?
It will never work.

CHAPTER 6:
A LOT OF FUSS
AND BOTHER

The Killers' debut album starts with swirling synths, helicopter rotor blades and keyboard blips that sound like Vince Clarke has fell asleep on the job. Then it's straight into the opener, 'Jenny Was A Friend Of Mine', the final part of the much-debated Killers murder mystery trilogy. Although it is unclear from the lyrics, it appears that the 'murderer' is under interrogation, probably from the police given that he states he has rights and resents having been there all day already. There is also a hint of good cop/bad cop with whispers in the ear after some harsh questioning. He is effectively constructing his alibi with this song. He switches from coolly aloof, almost baiting the interrogators, then turning to a frazzled, nervous suspect, sick of repeating his story over and over.

The murder appears to have taken place outside in the rain, and although Brandon has indeed hinted that water was involved in the death, it is not clear exactly how Jenny met her grisly end – perhaps soon after their row on the promenade? But there is no confession, instead an impassioned plea that he had no motive for killing her. She was, after all, a friend of his.

Sonically, the two most striking sounds you notice when you play this song for the first time is Brandon's voice and the synth phrases. While he recounts his relationship, the anxiety in Brandon's vocal is tangible even before the very first chorus; and swathes of utterly Eighties keyboards soak the background as he tells his tale. Listening to the clarity of this delivery and the way he is singing a melody, it sounds like he is simply having

The murder appears to have taken place outside in the rain, although Brandon has hinted that water was involved in the death.

some conspiratorial conversation in the corner of a dark, smokey pub. Facile as it sounds, you just know that despite the keyboard-laden backdrop, this guy on vocals doesn't look like Howard Jones. There seems almost a detached English tone to his voice, not surprising perhaps given the musical influences on display here, but it is mixed expertly with lacerating wails at the end of each chorus.

Mark is immediately on fine form too, combining stabbing riffs at the top of the bass neck with thumping rhythm bombs near the bottom. It is this snaking approach that is layered over Keuning's jagged rhythm guitar chords which underline and stabilise the complexities found elsewhere in the track.

The closing keyboard solo, an infectious riff that

Then comes the song that every band out there is looking for, the one single tune that changes their lives forever.

many bands would have made an entire song out of, notifies the listener that here is a band who are not content to fill one song with one hook. 'Jenny ...' is a blinding album opener.

Then comes the song that every band out there is looking for, the one single tune that changes their lives forever, the song that suddenly sees phonecalls being returned, venues chasing gigs, record labels buying lunch and magazines hunting interviews: 'Mr Brightside'. Probably the one song that The Killers will always be expected to play – and by their own choice the only song they have played at every gig, as mentioned.

In the context of this album, it's fizzing opening riff ups the ante after the blistering start of 'Jenny …' To note that it was one of the very first songs they wrote back in the day is astounding and merely confirms the suspicion that here is a band whose creative chemistry is of the ilk that separates great bands from merely good ones.

A hidden gem in this track is Ronnie's drumming. Listen to the cymbal work, relentless yet never intrusive; he keeps the snare functional yet strong; and his racing hi-hat skates along in the intro, almost out of

A hidden gem in this track is Ronnie's drumming, almost out of control like the green-eyed monster chewing up Mr Brightside.

control like the green-eyed monster that is chewing up Mr Brightside himself.

Then it's relentlessly on to 'Smile Like You Mean It'. From the opening keyboard riff, you can almost smell the Eighties, you can see David Bowie walking along the beach in *that* video, you can recall Steve Strange's make-up and Depeche Mode's blossoming global might. Again, Ronnie drives the song, thundering his snare drum as if he wants to snap the skin and sprinting along on that (surely tired out) hi-hat; Brandon's lead keyboard riff is the crux of the song though, the undoubted highlight and yet another hook. The vocal in the verse is perhaps a little dry, occasionally sounding diluted, but with so much else going on it is easy not to notice. Dave and Mark are relative by-standers until the later guitar riff which is straight out of early-era U2 live shows, recalling the Red Rocks that lie so close to The Killers home city. The brevity of the lyrics – like many Killers songs – is a welcome respite from the crammed songs of many contemporaries and its deft construction reinforces the feeling that here is an album of real substance. Although it is impossible to follow a song like 'Mr Brightside' without sounding slightly inferior, this third track easily maintains the enviable momentum that The Killers have captured right from the opening song of the album. You can't help thinking, 'we must be due a bad track by now?'

Wrong. In fact, at the risk of upsetting all the 'Mr Brightside' devotees out there (and there are millions of those), what's next is actually *the album's best song*: 'Somebody Told Me'. There, I've said it now. But I think it is, honest I do.

Brandon has gone on record as saying the fantastic first line of the cheeky chorus is "a great icebreaker. I think of it as the ultimate pick-up line. If I was a girl I would think that it's very clever, if a boy came up to me and said that … I think the girl would melt." Most girls would probably melt for Brandon Flowers even if he said, "you look like a bloke" to be honest, but that's splitting hairs.

This song has everything you could want in a pop song. A crescendo start, riffing guitars, swirling keyboards, thumping, strolling bass, thunderous drums, the lot. Somebody said this song was like "the Strokes gone disco" but, as much as I love Julian's band, this does not do justice to 'Somebody ...' which would surely stand head-and-shoulders above anything on that New York garage band's impressive back-catalogue.

The song is a simple premise, one of trying to meet someone in a nightclub. "It could be a strip club or a dance club," explained Brandon. Given his Bowie predilection, the androgynous looks of the boyfriend are entirely fitting. "It's really just a play on words," said Brandon. "But it gets people confused. That's good ... The androgyny means we appeal to boys and girls. That's really important to us."

Talking about 'Somebody Told Me', Brandon wisely avoided any temptation to delve into sexual ambiguity: "I'm not gay. I can't even be bothered to start some kind of intrigue about it," he says. "Bowie could nurture that sort of mystique, but this is an age where everyone knows everything about you in ten seconds."

But, despite the brilliant lyrics, superb bustling vocal delivery and compelling wave after wave of synthesizers, this song is actually most indebted to Ronnie Vannucci. In easily his most accomplished performance on *Hot Fuss*, he dominates and controls the song impeccably. Tom rolls, snare fills, hi-hat acrobatics and punchy double-hits to blast the chorus into view. Once you've heard him opening and closing the hi-hat in the chorus as Brandon sings about the androgynous boyfriend, you understand why that section stomps along with such ease. In the video, set against a huge neon TV screen in a Nevadian desert-scape. Ronnie's rendition of this song gives some hint as to the complexities and skill involved in his role in this song.

The song is a simple premise, one of trying to meet someone in a nightclub. "It's really just a play on words," said Brandon. "But it gets people confused. That's good ... the androgyny means we appeal to boys and girls. That's really important to us."

If you are thinking of starting playing the drums, or indeed if you already do, this is what it is all about. Better even than 'Mr Brightside'? You bet.

I think the next song is pants. I really do. The church piano and vague, minor chord intro with fairly weedy vocals on 'All These Things That I've Done' just don't work for me personally. I'm in the minority of course, and The Killers themselves will scoff at my ignorance – they have repeatedly said that this song is one that during concerts always seems to be able to lift the gig up another level – indeed, at Glasto in 2004 this song *on its own* vied for the gong for performance of the weekend. Fans will disagree too, but for me it feels too singalong, too camp and chirpy and just not as compelling as the four predecessors. Dave's guitar line is, for once, not utterly scintillating, and the rest of the instruments just sound like they are doing their job. The damped guitar chords and then the 'soul/soldier' refrain almost sound like twelve-bar blues, a worrying fact not helped by the gospel choir in for the party.

'Andy, You're A Star' is clanking, robotic, almost Kraftwerk in its brutal intro, yet it evolves backwards past the Seventies and into the hippy Sixties. Brandon's vocals have just a smidgen of treatment in them while the keyboards washing underneath the mix remind us heavily of Depeche Mode. The song was believed by many observers – wrongly – to be a confession of gay love. Brandon makes the rather cutting and, if you think about it obvious, defence that Andy could easily be a girl.

He was also inspired by "a football player from my high school," explained Brandon in *NME*. "Teachers favour the football players and wrestlers. It's made known: these guys are special. In fact, the teachers encouraged the hierarchy, as a lot of them were coaches too." The song is narrated by a loner who watches the all-rounder from afar and grows obsessed/jealous of his achievements/popularity and love life. An interesting premise and you can't help wondering if some of The Killers ever watched the muscle-bound sports stars at school; that said, if the realisation that none of them were ever likely to make the first team sent them back to band practice, then it could only have been a good thing!

One of the few criticisms of the album in the media was that the first half was blistering and the second, er, wasn't. It's a fair observation, but the real issue is that when you have a quartet of songs as brilliant as the opening four on *Hot Fuss*, to maintain that momentum is nigh on impossible. 'Andy ...' grows into an interesting very Bowie-esque chant, they keep it simple and the song works. But it is in mighty company so the stakes are very high.

Thankfully, the pace picks up again with 'On Top' with its pure Yazoo/Depeche Mode intro. You can almost hear two million teenage Killers fans practising this line on their shiny new keyboards ... such was

The song is narrated by a loner who watches the all-rounder from afar and grows obsessed/jealous of his achievements/popularity and love life.

a generation of synth heroes born. The band is back on form with 'On Top', Brandon in particular. Dave's guitar is almost acoustic, very gentle and controlled, interspersed with the lead keyboards which could be described as Butlins-meets-Bowie. To use his own words, Brandon's lyrics have a certain 'shimmy' about them and the whole effect is dazzling, camp, entertaining and infectious. By the time the keyboard lead line mixes effortlessly with the blazing synth chord sequence and finally Dave's piercing three-note guitar ripples, you could be in the corner of an Eighties disco at school or a youth club, white shoes and jackets in full effect and too much cider in the belly.

Cranking up the quality again is the eighth track, the fantastic 'Glamorous Indie Rock & Roll'. The drums are metronomic, clockwork, never failing, yet they somehow avoid the song lapsing into some cod-Kraftwerk tribute. In an age when labels are everything and those too-cool-for-the-room fall on the sword of the latest fashion/genre, there is something magnificently unashamed and proud about the titular declaration. 'Indie' as a term was absolutely of the Eighties; of course, it is still bandied about now, but there has been so much semantic and musical fragmentation since those heady days that the word is almost sterilised – in the same way that the word 'punk' has often come to mean all things to all men (for the record and by way of example, Busted, bless them – I bought the album and my little boy loves it – were not punk). Yet here is Brandon declaring his love for 'indie'. Take it or leave it. Hats off to him. What's more, it's not the grubby, baggy, long-haired, floppy-fringed, heads-down, shoe-gazing indie of yesteryear, it's 'glamorous', make-up drenched, dinner-jacket-wearing, rhinestone-covered, tight-trouser-wearing indie. Hurrah!

The song does sound a little stunted towards the end, with the wailing vocals and plodding rhythm, but by then we have been won back over by the record – and not least Mark's brilliant bass playing, more about which shortly.

Then, suddenly, bang! we are wrenched back to the heady heights of the album's first four songs with the shivering beauty of 'Believe Me, Natalie'. Hitchcock-like strings and a wavering keyboard akin to Orchestral Manoeuvres In The Dark bring in a captivating tumbling drum pattern, then Dave's repetitive two-chord guitar motif crashes in, very Edge-like, very emotional, a great start to this track.

The first verse and chorus are exquisite, brilliant pop music beautifully delivered; but then swooning into the second verse with achingly subtle synth takes the song another notch altogether. Again, the band seem to be looking for melodies and hooks at every turn, yet somehow appear capable of never over-dressing a song.

Then, suddenly, bang! we are wrenched back to the heady heights of the album's first four songs with the shivering beauty of 'Believe Me, Natalie'.

The middle-eight after the second chorus contradicts this point somewhat, its jarring edge and strange sound not quite fitting, but fortunately it is a brief diversion from the main feel-good excitement and genuine buoyancy of the main song. It somehow reminds me of The Cure's 'Friday I'm In Love' with its snatchy trumpets and escalation of good vibes. All those times listening to *The Head On The Door* when he was a kid were now paying off.

The song is actually about a party animal girl who ultimately catches the HIV virus from a dirty needle and succumbs to death through an AIDS-related illness. It's a tragedy that is brutally harsh coming amidst such a fragrant musical backdrop, but that makes the impact all the more powerful. One of the album's finest moments, unquestionably.

Much has been made of The Killers public ambition to knock U2 off their perch. Well, the very next song, 'Midnight Show' could come straight out of the Irish band's set in the late Eighties. The simple thumping bass is uncannily like Adam Clayton and the caustic guitar

"It's OK making the decision to split up," explained Brandon, "but when somebody finds somebody else, it's terrible; it's the worst feeling in the world." The closing chord sequence is a nice touch, a sad end to a very sad song.

solos and scratchy chords are pure Edge-inspired. Even Brandon's vocals ape Bono, especially the chorus' wail and the high notes not unlike 'New Year's Day'. Speaking of which, Dave's guitar solo in the centre of the song could almost have been in that song itself, yet at the same time it is all done with a Killers veneer.

This is the second song from the supposed murder trilogy, in which the woman victim finds her new man, the narrator discovers this and is enraged with jealousy and betrayal, starting the slippery spiral that leads to her murder. "It's OK making the decision to split up," explained Brandon, "but when somebody finds somebody else, it's terrible; it's the worst feeling in the world." The closing chord sequence is a nice touch, a sad end to a very sad song.

Then, finally, 'Everything Will Be Alright' has the unenviable task of closing out one of the finest debut albums for many years. What is a great shame is it is actually the worst song on the record. There's not much to say really, it seems so uncharitable after such an amazing record to finish on a bum note, literally.

Of course, the majority of the attention and acclaim inevitably lands on the frontman Brandon. But I'd like to look at other aspects of the record that deserve another listen. On 'Glamorous Indie Rock & Roll' Mark Stoermer's melodic talent really comes to the fore. You might say there is a hefty influence of Sting's dextrous bass playing from very early Police material, but the final result is entirely Mark's. "I feel that bass is a half percussion instrument and half melodic instrument," he explained. "It's best when it fits right in the middle, but still gives something interesting to the listener." Mark has the ability to lay down essentially lead melodies – most notably in the verses – pulling a song through its paces while never actually taking over or dominating the actual lead instruments of vocal and guitar/keyboards. Yet, Mark understands that bass and drums are there first and foremost for rhythm, which is why on most choruses he seems happy to fade into this more linear, background role. Using his pick, a distortion pedal and the occasional reduction in treble, Mark is able to dip in and out of a song's headlines with consummate ease. If you can put the keyboards to one side for a moment, listen to *Hot Fuss* again only checking out the bass lines and you will hear what I am saying. It is a remarkable performance.

Likewise, Dave Keuning has a very simple set-up, using only a Les Paul Custom and a Fender Hot Rod Deville. Although he will no doubt now have the world's guitar manufacturers throwing their products at his feet, he firmly believes it is easy to complicate matters and lose the focus of a song: "If it sounded good when you came up with it on a particular guitar," he told *Total Guitar*, "then you should play it on that particular guitar. I've done that several times; I've written this cool riff on the Strat and thought, 'I'll just play it on the Les Paul.' But then all the bite's gone."

Then there is Ronnie. Stylistically, he must be the nearest musical descendant of The Who's Keith Moon in modern rock. Their personal lives could not be more different, of course: Moon's drug taking, partying and eccentric behaviour are the stuff of rock and roll myth; Ronnie is a clean-living, hard-working and says Animal from *The Muppet Show* is one of his idols.

Quite unlike some Moon-esque rock and roll caricature, Ronnie has, according to Dave, "a weird thing about fresh air. He almost always has to have a window open. If we're in a car, or a bus, or a hotel room. Almost claustrophobic. For instance, we take turns with who we stay with in a hotel room, and when I'm with

Ronnie, he's gotta have a window open. Even if it's the middle of winter. And it kinda bugs me, but I can't really say anything because it's just a weird phobia."

However, watching Ronnie play live, you can't help but feel there is a slither of Keith Moon at work. He attacks the kit with vigour, and has the peculiar half-standing gait when striking the skins, especially when reaching for the cymbals. He also opens his mouth, grimaces, smiles and generally *performs* while playing

Then there is Ronnie. Stylistically, he must be the nearest musical descendant of The Who's Keith Moon in modern rock. Their personal lives could not be more different, of course.

some very complex drum patterns. Like, Mark, he knows when to withdraw and this allows many Killers' songs to open up and feel very spatial, right before he crashes back in and suddenly everything sounds epic. For me, he is the most entertaining member of the band to watch, maybe not the front man, the pin-up or the obvious crowd-pleaser, but he is captivating. Not least when he closes a set by standing on his bass drum and hammering seven bells out of his cymbals, as he did in front of a watching US record industry at the CMJ event that would ultimately see them sign a mega-bucks US record deal.

THE KILLERS

It is perhaps no surprise, then, to hear Ronnie talk of his influences: "I look up to a lot of older drummers," he told *www.worldwithoutborders*. "I first started out by getting into a lot of drummers like Buddy Rich, Gene Krupa, Joe Jones and other jazz drummers alike. Of course, I went into my rock and roll phases – particularly Sixties rock and roll – like Keith Moon, John Bonham, Mitch Mitchell, who is probably one of my favourite drummers from that era."

There is no question in my mind that this record is one of the best debut pop records of all time. *Hot Fuss* is that good. But then, The Killers don't need me to say that. After a modest start, *Hot Fuss* would stay in the UK's album charts for months on end, ultimately hitting the top spot for weeks.

They've sold four million copies already.

CHAPTER 7: A FIELD CHANGES EVERYTHING

"The Killers threaten to pry dance rock from the steely grip of hipsterdom and thrust it unrepentantly into the mainstream."
Rolling Stone

It is interesting to note that ahead of *Hot Fuss* being critically lauded at numerous end-of-year awards and sales figures shooting into the millions, the initial press reaction was actually quite modest. Good reviews were aplenty, but certain sectors were surprisingly only moderately impressed.

Perhaps surprisingly, *NME* only put *Hot Fuss* as their thirteenth best album of the year; Brandon was only their eighth 'Coolest' person [junkie rock star Pete Doherty was controversially their top choice]; and most strangely of all, 'Somebody Told Me' was a pitiful Number 34 in their 'Singles of the Year' category. At least they were being objective, rather than printing the fawning press that ultimately does a band little or no good.

However, of all the factors that turned The Killers from an exciting new band into one of the world's biggest, one single live performance can be highlighted as absolutely crucial: Glastonbury 2004.

Rain, mud, Oasis, Paul McCartney and Muse headlining on the Pyramid stage ... and The Killers nestled quietly in the New Bands Tent. Or at least everyone thought it was going to be quiet. It actually turned into what remains to this day the single most important show of the band's young life.

With word of mouth on the band at fever pitch, The Killers were in that odd position of being talked about widely even though they hadn't actually achieved anything yet. The New Bands Tent can be a difficult proving ground for some acts, as it is usually tucked away on the site and some acts find it hard to drag the happy campers away from the established names on the main stage. Much of the day in this secondary tent sees new bands perform to a half-filled arena.

When The Killers walked on stage that day, however, the tent was already bulging at the seams and there were punters eighty deep *outside* too. Without doubt the band could have easily played a show on the main stage, but in terms of sheer hype, it was probably ideal that this debut Glasto show was on such a small stage. It was their performance of a lifetime.

Lizard King personnel were there to see their new protégés and could barely contain their excitement. Talking to *Hot Press* magazine, that label's Siona Ryan

When The Killers walked on stage that day, however, the tent was already bulging at the seams and there were punters eighty deep outside too.

revealed that, "I'd hoped [the gig would work] but didn't know for sure until about twenty minutes beforehand when we were backstage and saw thousands and thousands of people bee-lining for the New Bands Tent ... I remember Ronnie and Brandon laughing at us afterwards because we were so overwhelmed. The word of mouth had really tipped over." For Lizard King, hearing thousands of Glasto fans cheering along to the songs was a massive moment.

The press agreed. *NME* said they were "energetic, synthy, hit-packed, sweaty and bloody brilliant." Nonetheless, it remained pertinent in the light of later events that the band's entire Glasto coverage was limited to 28 words in *NME*. The Killers performance was the main surprise of the weekend and changed everything for them. One year later they would be offered the headline slot on the main stage.

With this Glasto triumph under their belts, he only way was up for The Killers. As has been mentioned, the UK was the first territory to take up The Killers call to (ch)arms. By the summer of 2005, *Hot Fuss* had spent months in the UK's album charts and sold in excess of one million copies. That's one in every 25 adults. Take away fans of Celine Dion, Robbie Williams and Daniel O'Donnell and that's getting on for one in every ten.

Once America had finally come on board, amidst US DJs claiming 'you heard it here first', the band's sales stats rocketed. At first, with *Hot Fuss* going platinum in the UK for 300,000 sales, the US trailed behind at just 50,000. Then 100,000. Then half a million. At the time of writing, the album has shifted in excess of two million copies in the US alone. That's three million with the UK, double that with Europe and thirty-eight more copies if you include Paraguay. It wasn't just album sales that gave you an indication of their popularity. When *NME* offered to put readers' questions to the band, over *one thousand* people wrote in. That's a lot of stamps.

The band was very clever too in the way they promoted the record. Tons of gigs were a given, they never came off the road and this work ethic is often overlooked by critics eager to dismiss them as made-up, glamour pop lightweights. Not true, look at their touring schedules, there's nothing lightweight about that.

While it was the Glasto show that truly propelled The Killers on to an altogether new level of fame in the UK, this specific show was backed up mightily by similarly massive performances at other UK summer festivals. At the ever-popular V Festival, organised across two days and two venues in August, they met with such a rapturous reception at both shows that by the time they came to sign records, T-shirts and other stuff for the fans in the Signing Tent, they hastily delivered an impromptu performance! Shooting off south down the M1 they signed for hundreds of fans again at the city's key Virgin

In addition to the relentless touring, the band released a batch of brilliant singles, always interestingly formatted too, with coloured vinyl, unusual B-sides/mixes, that just kept revitalising sales of Hot Fuss.

Megastore before playing a blinding show at the Kentish Town Forum.

In addition to the relentless touring, the band released a batch of brilliant singles, always interestingly formatted too, with coloured vinyl, unusual B-sides/mixes, that just kept revitalising sales of *Hot Fuss*. They even made the album available in sky blue vinyl in a limited edition. Later, in the summer of 2005, another intriguing special edition would also be made available which included three 'bonus' tracks, namely 'Glamorous Indie Rock & Roll', 'The Ballad of Michael Valentine' and 'Under The Gun' along with previously unseen artwork.

But it was the great singles that kept fuelling the fire most of all. The August 2004 release of 'All These Things That I've Done' was like a shot in the arm of the album, sending it back up the charts as some radio stations added them to their playlists for the first time, venues sold out tickets and music television placed them on heavy rotation.

The clip for 'All These Things That I've Done' was, however, also pants. It was filmed in the East End of London in Brick Lane, an area famous for its curry houses and home to the popular annual curry festival. With the other singles featuring very moody and 'cool' promos, Brandon explained how the band wanted to "just make a really happy video. When we thought about it, we realised that there aren't that many positive-feeling videos, and the world needs more happy videos. This song is really uplifting and we wanted something that would portray that."

In the clip, the band walk along Brick Lane and are gradually joined by more and more fans, singing as they go, until they are finally joined by a gospel choir for the final refrain of the track [they had performed this track at the spring 2004 Coachella Festival with the Mt. Cavalry Holy Church gospel choir]. Some of the extras were from casting agencies, a few were genuine fans and there were even a few neighbours thrown in (everybody needs good neighbours). Unfortunately, it didn't work. The weakest song on the album with a weak video. And gospel choirs are hard to pull off unless you are Bono or Jay-Z. But that's just me talking. Most people disagreed and the video enjoyed generous airplay on TV and helped fling the single up to Number 18 in the charts in late August. Sales were almost half of the preceding single which might have been a worry for the band but they pressed on regardless.

Some consolation could later be gleaned in early 2005 when *NME* awarded the band three trophies at its annual ceremony in February, including 'Best International Band' (ahead of U2), 'Best Dressed' and 'Sexiest Man'. Speaking to the crowd during his acceptance speech, Brandon said, "We're very excited to win this award. This band is comprised of three boys who weren't afraid to dream big ... and one gentle giant."

Of course, there are always the dissenters and in the case of The Killers, they found one very well-educated doubter in the form of Germaine Greer, superbrain, legendary feminist writer and, oddly, recent participant of spell in the *Celebrity Big Brother* house. She described the band as, "dreary, bankrupt [and] infantile." Not that The Killers need worry, with reports quoting Elton John and David Bowie as big fans.

By the autumn of 2004, momentum in the UK was now so enormous that their scheduled shows had to be elevated to some of the country's biggest venues. For their November dates, The Killers played at places such as the Manchester Academy and the legendary

Shepherds Bush Empire.

Also, while they were only just starting to get high profile TV appearances in the US (such as *The Conan O'Brien Show*), The Killers were already at the top of the tree with regard to UK entertainment shows. Comedian and top presenter Jonathan Ross had single-handedly revived the chat show format in Britain after it had threatened to fall into terminal decline with the musty and past-its-welcome failings of the once legendary *Parkinson* format. Ross was crude, rude and baited his guests mercilessly. Fortunately, The Killers only had to hang around backstage and then perform one song, so they avoided his sharpened tongue. In the green room – which was filmed live for much of the show – they found themselves in the quite surreal situation of sitting next to Ginger Spice and Buffy The Vampire Slayer. It wouldn't be until April 2005 that they finally got invited on to the US equivalent, *The Tonight Show With Jay Leno*. By then, they would be one of the biggest bands in the world.

"We've got one goal – to stick around, and we will ... for a long time."
Brandon Flowers

The UK's music media and journalists are a much-maligned bunch. Subject to any stinging reviews they might give this book, their recent track record of breaking big bands seems completely at odds with the mythology that they repeatedly hail 'the best new band' only for said outfit to disappear without trace. The now-defunct *Melody Maker* famously heralded Suede as exactly that, and Brett Andersen *et al* duly delivered, pre-empting Britpop by two years with their divine 'Animal Nitrate' single. Gay Dad were not so lucky and sank fast. It's a high risk business.

However, in more recent times, the British music press have seemed adept at picking out the pearls among the swine. In doing so, they have played a very key role

In the green room – which was filmed live for much of the show – they found themselves in the quite surreal situation of sitting next to Ginger Spice and Buffy The Vampire Slayer.

in breaking new bands from America over here in the UK first, before watching (surely with some pride) as that band then returns to the US as conquering heroes and finally wins over their home market.

Two obvious examples are The Strokes and The White Stripes. The former of these two bands was initially the most commercially successful of this unlikely duo. Sporting pretty boy looks, Velvet Underground overtones and pseudo-garage rock songs, The Strokes utterly seduced the British rock press in 2001 with their debut album *Is This It* [high on fashion and life, low on question marks] and subsequent blinding live shows. The adulation heaped on the band in the UK had not been seen since the breakthrough days of Oasis and it was easy to see why. Lead singer Julian Casablancas led a gang of *Les Desireables* that boasted private school education, famous and wealthy parents, hell, even stylish *names* – and fortunately a volley of sharp, biting and yet brutally simple rock songs. Despite the obvious New York/Velvet Underground/Television etc connection, however, the US market was not immediately enamoured with the band – even though all their very early shows were performed in and around the Big Apple. It took a record deal with the UK's Rough

You don't need to ache for a revolution to be pissed off; it might just be that you are a jealous freak … Mr Brightside, you know who we are talking about.

Trade label and festival headline slots in England before the American music listener finally started to sit up and take notice (ironically just as their second album was struggling to win over the critics back in the UK). Once again, the British music media had been the first to hail the new arrivals.

Although only a deaf man with cheese in his ears would suggest The Killers sound like The Strokes, some observers have nonetheless linked the vocal style of

Brandon with that of Strokes' frontman Julian Casablancas. There are some similarities: both sing notes that could sound like flat incidentals, both use a very staccato delivery and both sound, at times, very pissed off. Yet it's hard to think either singer carries a burning social discontent within their soul, not least for Casablancas who comes from a very privileged background. Yet, the disaffection is there and, vocally at least, it works. You don't need to ache for a revolution to be pissed off; it might just be that you are a jealous freak ... Mr Brightside, you know who we are talking about. For those critics who demean both bands for not having genuine social change in their bones, change the record.

But to get back to the point regarding UK/US success, The Strokes' path crossed with Detroit's The White Stripes on a 'co-headlining' series of dates in the summer of 2002. Jack and Meg White's brother-sister/husband-wife duo (er, ex-husband, ex-wife actually) had equally enthralled the British music press. The entrenched blues ethos of their music and the exaggerated mystique of their history often masked the real creative crux of the band – Jack's scintillating guitar work and purist songwriting blended with Meg's brilliantly simple drumming – but the UK public understood the appeal. Again, at first, the USA did not concur and the duo found themselves unable to walk the streets of London in peace while back in Motor City they were just another band in search of success. That all changed of course, most notably with their fourth album

Elephant, but it was just another example of the British music press getting it *right* (Scissor Sisters would soon come roaring through on the back of ecstatic UK press attention too).

And so to The Killers. The best British band to come out of America in years. It made altogether more sense that a group weaned on a diet of Morrissey, Depeche Mode, The Cure and so on, first made an impression among the green fields and winding country lanes of England. Ronnie's old friend PJ Perez was certainly surprised when he saw just how massive the band were in the UK; having noted their 'farewell' show in Vegas was to about three hundred people, he thought at first that their absence from the Vegas scene was terminal. "They then disappeared," he told Stuart Clark of *Hot Press* magazine, "which I took as a sign that they'd broken up. I discovered otherwise three or four months later when I ran into Ronnie ... Things after that took off real quick."

Rooting out why The Killers fitted in to British music when they did is only half the story; it is equally important to define why they *didn't* fit into the tastes of their native land at the time too. The years 2003 and 2004 were not exactly a hotbed of Eighties retro music. In America at least, the delay in The Killers hitting the big time may partly have been to do with the state of the nation, so to speak, with regard to music taste. Hip-hop and R&B had developed from an underground genre that was largely ignored by radio and music television into the dominant genre in world music. By 2004, only

6% of American youth were listening to rock radio at any given moment; more than 20% of the same demograph were listening to hip-hop/R&B stations. The situation was so severe that several high profile rock stations actually closed down.

Nu-metal had been strangled from within by the more demanding likes of System Of A Down; punk was about to re-emerge with the genre's first punk rock opera, Green Day's multi-million-selling *American Idiot* and pop was struggling, as Britney went haywire and Christina got 'dirrty'. So it was against this backdrop of changing musical taste that The Killers were fighting. This wasn't the only reason that it took them time to hit paydirt in the US of course – myopic record labels is another obvious factor – but it is an interesting environment for a band so immersed in British influences and rock music to strive. There seemed little room for a bunch of Las Vegas tunesmiths, wearing make-up and suits and redefining and remoulding the decade of big hair, big shoulder-pads and Loadsamoney.

But redefine it they did and there is one over-riding reason why. It wasn't the fashion, it wasn't major label money, it wasn't even Brandon's undoubtedly good looks.

It was because *they had the songs*.

The Killers have really excelled in their ability to avoid the 'retro' tag. Others haven't been so lucky, or perhaps so talented. The cyclical nature of music, fashion, art and the media cannot be denied of course, and short of going back to cavemen banging sticks and drums you could take pretty much any new band and trace their genealogical roots.

Not surprisingly, The Killers became rather weary of discussing the 'Eighties or not?' debate. "The Eighties thing, it's a small part of what we make up," Mark told Samantha Hall. "We're influenced by so many bands – Pink Floyd, The Who, Seventies bands too; I think people need to have everything pigeonholed so they can get their head round the influx of new music."

Kaiser Chiefs offer some witty dittys, to be sure, but Damon Albarn and his fellow Blur boys must struggle to avoid a wry smile when they see the Fred Perry's and drainpipe jeans and hear the decidedly *Parklife*-esque tunes; The Bravery, fine boys I am sure and I don't know them personally so bear that in mind, but their music is

Not surprisingly, The Killers became rather weary of discussing the 'Eighties or not?' debate. "The Eighties thing, it's a small part of what we make up."

like a bag of old vinyl melted down into a pot and poured out on to a CD pressing machine; Australia's Jet are surely the worst example, treading the wrong side of a very thin line between being influenced and being just a tribute … and a bad one at that.

Similarly, many of these bands are appealing to fans

who bought the originals first time around. Not exclusively, but a substantial percentage of their fan base will be older listeners reliving a nostalgia trip. Where The Killers make a ... er ... killing is the fact that

My niece Emily is one such fan. She's just turned sixteen and is into graffiti, emo, Kerrang!, downloads, fashion and ... The Killers.

they appeal to a very young generation to whom Depeche Mode sounds like a shortcut on your i-Pod and Strawberry Switchblade sounds like a Pick 'n' Mix.

My niece Emily is one such fan. She's just turned sixteen and is into graffiti, emo, *Kerrang!*, downloads, fashion and ... The Killers. Mention any of the band's revered 'influences' and she will know exactly who you are talking about, even though most of them pre-date her birth. But it will (usually) be a Killers CD she puts on before a Depeche Mode one. She loves Brandon Flowers, the songs, the outfits, the songs, the gigs, the songs ... you get the picture. Her ideal gig would be Funeral For A Friend and The Killers (and maybe System Of A Down for her brother James). That is why Brandon and his chums have sold four million albums, not because there are echoes of The Cure or slithers that remind you of Bowie. The Killers appeal to the i-Podowning, Playstation-thumbing, camera-phone carrying, SMS texting generation *en masse*. They are a very modern band, make no mistake.

CHAPTER 8: MY LIFE IN POP MUSIC

"I'll sleep at night as long as we don't lose to Hoobastank."
Dave Keuning just prior to the Grammy Awards, 2005.

Once The Killers had broken through, the climate in 2005 in particular was very much in their favour. Coldplay had released their much-anticipated third album, *X&Y*, which sold about a trillion copies in a week; System Of A Down and Green Day were selling more records and tickets than major pop artists like

Madonna; bands such as My Chemical Romance were dominating magazine covers and music channels; and The Killers suddenly found themselves lauded by various hip-hop and R&B names, such as Jay-Z and P Diddy.

"Rock will always be here," said Ric Rubin, mega-famous producer and record label mogul. Unfortunately, much of the recording industry has turned away from rock, and I'm not exactly sure why. [But] there's a misconception that the big pop and hip-hop albums sell more than the big rock records."

Brandon seemed aware of the shifting face of commercial music, when he spoke to Nicole Roberge of *Soundwaves* magazine: "The radio's changing and to be one of the bands that's helping do that will forever be something we're proud of. Even if it just lasts a while. It's hard right now because some rock stations are shutting down and we're lucky because we've crossed over to some pop stations. But it's gonna be difficult for new rock bands."

The extent to which rock was enjoying something of a revival can be seen in 2004's end of year award nominations. In the first week of December, 2004, The Killers were nominated for no less than three Grammy Awards. They received nods for 'Best Rock Album', 'Best Rock Song' ('Somebody Told Me'), and 'Best Rock Performance by Duo or Group with Vocal' ('Somebody Told Me'). In the 'Best Rock Album' they were up against Elvis Costello, Green Day, Velvet Revolver and Hoobastank. [it was a good year for music from their home city – fellow Vegas band The Crystal Method were nominated in the newly created 'Best Electronic/Dance Album category.]

Despite having got relatively used to the rarefied air of stardom in such a short space of time, the band were still shocked by these latest developments. Grammys were not something that anyone took lightly. Ronnie

"The radio's changing and to be one of the bands that's helping do that will forever be something we're proud of. It's hard right now because some rock stations are shutting down and we're lucky because we've crossed over to some pop stations."

Vannucci told *The Oregonian* how he found out: "I was coming out of the shower and my wife came busting in. 'You're nominated for a Grammy! You're nominated for Grammy!' It was like nine in the morning, and I thought that was crazy, I was like, 'No way.' It really hasn't sunk in yet."

Sadly, on the night they won bugger all.

Still, one of the hosts of the ceremony at Los Angeles' Staples Center, ace rapper Jay-Z, announced they were his favourite band so it wasn't all bad. Plus, in January 2005 their debut album had been certified platinum, recognising sales of more than one million copies in the USA alone.

They were also nominated for the 2004 Shortlist Prize, the American equivalent of the Mercury Prize (where if anyone has heard of you, you are guaranteed not to win). The award nominated ten acts for 'Achievement in Music' including alongside The Killers Air, Dizzee Rascal, Franz Ferdinand, The Streets and Ghostface Killah among others. The panel of judges has included over the years such luminaries as 3D from Massive Attack, the all-conquering Jack Black and, er, The Dixie Chicks. The winner was announced at a gala concert at Los Angeles' Wiltern Theater in November 2004. Sadly, on the night The Killers won bugger all.

Further critical acclaim was heaped on the band when the nominations for the prestigious Brit Awards were announced ahead of the February 2005 ceremony. The

He is, of course, a very good-looking chap, you would be churlish to deny that. He is a great singer, obviously. He writes cunning lyrics and deftly blends melody with words. Yet he is much more than the sum of his parts too.

Killers were put forward in the 'International Album' and 'International Breakthrough Act' categories. They were vying for the awards with the likes of the tediously dull Maroon 5, OutKast, the bizarre Elton John-style tribute act Scissor Sisters and that good old 'British' band, the Irish legends U2. Sadly, on the night they won bugger all.

At the centre (stage) of The Killers is Brandon Flowers. This band is very much a democracy and a strong gang, without a doubt, but Brandon is in many ways, the ace up their sleeve. He is, of course, a very good-looking chap, you would be churlish to deny that. He is a great singer, obviously. He writes cunning lyrics and deftly blends melody with words. Yet he is much more than the sum of his parts too. His band mate Mark has gone on record as saying that "the guy never faced rejection his whole life" (he's not asked me out for a meal yet). You can see this streak of unfettered self-confidence in the steely determination of his eyes, his proud jaw line and the way his head is always slightly cocked up, almost to guarantee that he can survey you from above. Even his band mates have noticed a change, as Dave told *Q* magazine: "Brandon's ego has definitely gone up, I will say that. And he loves what's happened to us. We all do, of course, but Brandon, well, Brandon more."

The modern pop star is so much more than just a good singer or performer and Brandon inherently understands this. He plays the media beautifully. He knows the buttons to press, the soundbites to deliver, the right time to criticise and the best time to revere. He understands the tangible benefits of image, of looks, of placing the right photo in the right magazine at the right time.

He is unashamed of the premise too – indeed he is

positively proud of his interest in the band's image. Bubbly discussing how he'd be keen to "do something with Dior [but] I wouldn't model though," he can happily talk about his favourite designers – Hedi Slimane for example – without a hint of irony and with his credibility intact.

Drawing on a European cigarette through cheekbones you could open a tin with, while wearing an *haute couture* label dinner jacket and lip-gloss is not a look that just anybody could pull off. But Brandon can, and does, with consummate ease. The key point is, although he puts endless energy into his/the band's presentation, he makes it look like he doesn't have to try.

This is how a post-Millennial pop star of longevity operates, and Brandon is up there with the very best of them. Has been since before he was a pop star. That's part of the reason why he is one, he knew how to do all this before he'd even had the opportunity to put it all into practice. "It's important to look good," he told *Q* magazine's Nick Duerden in mid-2005. "Great music is great music, but image is priceless. I'm not saying I'm in this position because I'm good-looking but it certainly helps."

Of course, being the front man comes with baggage, but Brandon seems all too aware of that responsibility. "It can be hard being the singer in a band," he told *NME*. "I've got a lot on my plate sometimes. It's something I knew would happen, it's just kind of how it is. Still, I hope I can make it … there are a lot of people who have made it through, like Bono." He still forgets his profile at times; on one trip to London in early 2005 he wanted to get the train out of London and would have done so had his record label not pointed out that he would probably have been mobbed within a hundred yards of their office.

Maybe one of the reasons that Brandon can carry off his role as lead singer with one of the world's biggest bands is that, by his own admission, it's not an act. "I always wanted people to know who I was. I don't think the Brandon Flowers you see on stage is that different to the everyday Brandon Flowers, I think we are pretty much the same."

"It can be hard being the singer in a band," he told NME. "I've got a lot on my plate sometimes. It's something I knew would happen, it's just kind of how it is."

Yet, tellingly for a pencil-thin front man, he was a chubby child and claims this has left him with lasting self-doubt about his image. Maybe he makes up for this supposed fragility with his air of supreme confidence or maybe he just looks in the mirror most mornings and says, as James Blunt implores, "You're beautiful."

Unusually for an American pop star, Brandon's teeth are very English: "It's an on going battle," he told *NME*. "Both of my parents have terrible teeth so I'm doomed. Ever since he was twenty my dad has had dentures, and my mum has every tooth capped."

One refreshing aspect of his approach is his disregard for the drug culture that infuses almost every square inch of rock and roll. With the rigours of a touring life endlessly spinning young braves into the clutches of soft and hard drugs, Brandon remains unmoved by the whole prospect. "It bothers me that I'd be more credible to certain people if I had a drug problem. Why? That's bullshit. I'm not interested in drugs because I've seen what they can do."

"People compare The Bravery to The Killers and The Bravery are offended. I took offence to that … they could have been more gracious about that."

He's also been quoted as saying, "I think we're the cleanest band in the world, next to the busiest. Maybe the two go hand in hand." Instead of snorting cocaine off prostitute's bottoms, as some rock stars are wont to do, The Killers prefer to go to the movies or the shops. Don't knock it, it worked for Coldplay.

Synonymous with self-confidence is the belief that you are better than most other people. Although he hasn't said as much, Brandon has made a name for himself for criticising other bands. He called fellow Americans Secret Machines "total assholes"; when Velvet Revolver were competing with The Killers at the Grammys for 'Best Rock Album', he said, "You've got the votes for Velvet Revolver based on who they are, which kind of sucks for us. I've heard all their singles, and I can't remember one of them." [For the record, Dave can turn his hand to the hilarious put-down when suitably moved – speaking after they came home empty-handed from the 2005 Brit Awards, he said, "Those pansies the Scissor Sisters got 'Best International Group'. We were robbed by a bunch of fairy boys."]

However, the most famous spat of all is with New York's The Bravery. Brandon was quoted as saying, "Look at a band like The Bravery, they're signed because we're a band. How can you say, 'My heart really belongs to what I do now,' but you used to be in a ska band." The Bravery did not take kindly to the insinuation that they got a record deal because of The Killers' success but Brandon was unmoved. In another interview, he expanded a little more on why there was such friction. "People compare The Bravery to The Killers and The Bravery are offended. I took offence to that. I mean, we sold them our van, they use our press people … we've done nothing but open doors for them. That's all we're saying – they could have been more gracious about that."

The Bravery's lead singer, Sam Endicott, did not shy away from the row, however, retorting that "The poor guy, he's scared. I feel bad talking about him because it's like hitting a girl. It's like picking on a kid in a wheelchair." Of Killers' bassist Matt he also said, "He looks like a little Dutch girl with a beard, but like a nine-foot-tall Dutch girl, like a mutant radioactive." Ow! Saucer of milk for table five.

THE KILLERS

The argument rumbled on for months and the music papers loved the tension, just as they had loved it when Oasis and Blur were at each other's throats ten years previous. And yet, with the cool air of someone who knows his band will come out on top, Brandon consigned the argument to the waste-paper bin by simply saying, "I've never actually said anything bad about anyone who didn't deserve it." In a way, you can't argue with that. Can you?

By now, The Killers were so popular that Brandon was increasingly coming into contact with his own heroes, so spats with contemporaries like this seemed all the more irrelevant. He is happy to go on record as saying that The Smiths' Morrissey is the single most important influence on him personally. He proudly boasts of reading every interview The Mozza has ever given, bought every record either with The Smiths or solo, seen him live countless times and just generally admired him from afar. On a later Killers UK tour, he even visited – albeit with the other four band members – The Holy Name Church in Manchester as mentioned in 'Vicar In A Tutu' and The Salford Lads Club made famous by Mozza. I wanna be adored indeed.

Unfortunately, years later when Brandon was in fact being adored himself by Killers fans all over the world, he was delighted to be asked to support Morrissey in LA. Barely able to contain his excitement for much of the day, Brandon was heading for a fall and he fell hard – when Mozza passed him backstage and ignored him.

"I was devastated," Brandon told *Q* magazine's Nick Duerden. "I read an interview with him in which he said Marc Bolan, his idol, did the very same thing to him years earlier and it crushed him. So why did he do that to me?" To be fair to Mozza, Brandon has also made reference to Morrissey watching the band soundcheck and regretting not waving at the former Smith, although he did admit to "putting on a show for him."

David Bowie famously went to see the band in New York at the city's Irving Plaza venue in 2004. The

> *"I went numb. I shook his hand and thought, 'You wrote 'Ashes To Ashes'.*
> *You're not supposed to like me. I still have David Bowie posters on my wall."*

usually super-cool Brandon was more than happy to admit that this was "a big deal". Afterwards, The Thin White Duke came to The Killers' dressing room and Brandon's choice of memory tells us much about his musical taste when confronted by the man most people remember as Ziggy. "I went numb. I shook his hand and thought, 'You wrote 'Ashes To Ashes'. You're not supposed to like me. I still have Bowie posters on my wall." Brandon also said, "I could see him the entire time. I was fucking dying, 'cause he's the one for me. I shook his hand, and he said, 'I felt like I just saw the history of rock and roll.' I think he was basically saying we rip off from every genre." In a nice way of course. [when the Grammy award-winning, Jacques Lu Cont remixed 'Mr Brightside' in early 2005, he called his incredible version the 'Thin White Duke Remix'.

Despite appearances to the contrary, Brandon was only a modest glam rock fan. He loved Bowie and T Rex's Marc Bolan, but does not claim to be a fanatic of either. "Watching *Top of the Pops* when [T Rex] did ['Metal Guru'], I was just looking at everybody dance. It just shows what a positive thing music can be."

CHAPTER 9:
LIVE AND
LET LIVE

"We set out to be like U2 and conquer the world. We think they're the biggest band in the world and we'd like to take they're place when they retire."
Mark Stoermer

Given the band's Eighties inclinations via influences such as Depeche Mode, it seemed entirely fitting that the director for what is easily their best video to date – the clip for the US-only release of 'All These Things That I've Done – was Anton Corbijn. Dutch-born Corbijn first made his name as one of rock's most sought-after photographers, with his iconic images adorning countless landmark records, such as U2's *Joshua Tree* and Depeche Mode's *Violator*. Moving quickly into music video, Corbijn seemed able to transfer his talent to celluloid, particularly his penchant for the surreal and symbolic. Although his association with the two former bands is well-known, Corbijn has also directed videos for, among others, Nirvana, the Rollins Band, Metallica, Red Hot Chili Peppers and, oddly, Naomi Campbell.

His clip for The Killers was actually his first such video work for two whole years, which in itself was a compliment to the band. It's full of busty cow-girls, boomerangs, Stetsons, neon signs and someone drowning in a puddle of water. Naturally. They were delighted: "We're very excited because Anton is someone we completely admire," Brandon told *www.amplifier.at*, "and he totally lived up to our expectations. He's a genius with his pictures and film, and he came up with a great concept."

Anton was equally complementary: "They are a great bunch of guys with a long-term vision. The song is just fantastic and we tried to make it into a pretty bizarre story for the video." Further, the industry whisper–mongerers would later pen Corbijn as the hot favourite to direct The Killers' oft-discussed long-form video, entitled *A Murder Trilogy*.

Arguably the best place to see The Killers' chemistry in action is at a gig. Despite their pretty boy reputation, this band are very heavy tourers. In 2004 alone they played over 200 shows. Being on the road is never a normal existence and the band are eager to avoid being cocooned in the pampered/exhausted life that heavy, high profile touring involves. "It's important to go home," Brandon told *NME*, "and be normal ... being on the road is so abnormal. You have people to get everything for you and that's weird."

Their biggest solo UK show to date came in February of 2005 when they headlined the cavernous Brixton Academy. The Shockwaves/*NME* tour with Kaiser Chiefs, The Futureheads and Bloc Party had finished at that venue on February 9 but by then it was clear that The Killers did not need any other bands on the bill to sell out the ticket allocation of close to 4000 people. Duly, a stand-alone show was booked for February 19 but this sold out in fifty minutes; faced with at least another 4000 people clamouring for tickets, the band booked a matinee performance for the same day. This too sold out within an hour. This was a serious indication that The Killers were now fast approaching becoming a stadium band. Unless their second album is a complete donkey, there seems little doubt that the next time they headline a tour of the UK, it will be in the nation's finest sheds.

Notably, it was at this Brixton headline slot that the band finally got to meet Noel Gallagher of Oasis, the band that had initially drawn Brandon and Dave together all that time ago through that Vegas classified ad. Dave was impressed: "He was cool. He's quite short and a little less mouthy than I expected. Do I rate him as a guitarist? ... He's better than basic. People should write a song like 'Don't Look Back In Anger' or come up with a riff as good as 'Champagne Supernova' then come back and say something." Of his other guitar heroes, he says he would like to meet Billy Corgan, Robert Smith and Johnny Marr. Too late for George Harrison and Hendrix sadly.

A string of very high profile UK festival slots in 2005 served the dual purpose of confirming just how good The Killers were as a live band but also their lofty status

"We didn't think we were deserving of a headlining slot, we're just happy to be playing in a good spot at Glastonbury anyway. We only have one album out."

as one of the biggest bands in the world. While some reviewers harshly suggested that having only one album under their belts meant their long festival sets at events such as Reading, Glastonbury and the like felt like 'all the hits' mixed in with substandard B-sides, the band themselves did acknowledge with admirable perspective how far they had come in such a short space of time. This was most poignantly highlighted when they were offered the headline slot at Glastonbury – ridiculous considering how young the band was, yet entirely appropriate considering their popularity and commercial success – and promptly and politely declined. The slot had only become available when Kylie Minogue had been given the awful diagnosis of breast cancer and naturally cancelled all such professional engagements while she went into treatment. Filling the void would have been an easy thing to do for the second-on-the-bill Killers but they were not to be tempted. As Ronnie told *NME*: "We didn't take it because we're basically a band that's been around for, as far as the UK's concerned, a little over a year. So we didn't think we were deserving of a headlining slot, we're just happy to be playing in a good spot at Glastonbury anyway. We only have one album out."

The set at Glasto itself was a corker… but according to some reports it nearly was a man short. The near-absence wasn't even Ronnie, who was suffering from food poisoning but refused to miss the show. With journalists as well as Brandon's brother Shane on board, The Killers' tour bus headed from their plush central London hotel towards Glastonbury, finally reassured that the reports of massive power failures at the rain-deluged site were under control and the show was still on. *Q* magazine bluntly stated that "Dave's temper is legendary" which was a worrying precursor to what was about to happen. They drove along the M4, stopping at Fleet Services for a hydrogenated vegetable oil meat slab (but not Brandon), then merrily hopped back on the bus and continued their journey.

Without Dave.

He was standing in the car park, no mobile phone,

very little money and no transport to a gig where 100,000 people were waiting with great excitement to hear his band. "If a group of us were walking down the street, it's always Dave who's trailing," said Brandon by way of affectionate explanation.

The bus returned after a phone call was made to the tour manager and Dave was picked up, crisis averted. It transpired that Dave initially fed all his spare change into a payphone to call the only number he thought could help – the band's US management. They were on

Just twelve chaotic months later and they found themselves second on the bill. Eighteen months earlier they had played to one hundred people at that early Dublin Castle gig. Now it was 100,000.

answer machine. Forced to asking passing strangers for change, Dave eventually got lucky after eight people hurriedly walked past him as if he wasn't there. Eventually he got through to the band's soundman – already at the Glasto site – and the disaster was avoided. A brief tourist stop at Stonehenge calmed the nerves and the band were on their way.

Brandon wore a minty white/green dinner jacket and painfully tight black trousers (the green jacket was "saved for Glastonbury it's a very green festival so it works"). He's a good-looking fella, no doubt about that, but those drainpipe trousers are not a good look. It was, nonetheless, a brave choice of outfit, not because it highlighted his rather thin legs but because Glasto is as well known for its mud as it is for its music.

The Killers had only heard of the marathon Glasto weekend in 2001 after reading a review in a UK magazine, so by the time they played in the 'New Bands Tent' in 2004, they were very pleased to be part of the myth. Just twelve chaotic months later and they found themselves *second on the bill*. Eighteen months earlier they had played to one hundred people at that early Dublin Castle gig. Now it was 100,000. Although the headliners' Pyramid Stage might mirror the preposterous but fantastic Luxor Hotel in their hometown of Vegas, given the meteoric rise you could forgive them if they suffered from a case of the Glastonbury bends.

Although the UK's music press had backed The Killers heartily thus far in their career, there were reviews of Glastonbury that were not exactly positive. *NME*, a magazine that had generously awarded the band column feet rather than inches for nearly two years now, were less than impressed with certain aspects of the show. Their reviewer Barry Nicolson said, "When the weather's this grim the muddied masses need something to connect with, not some poseur whose aloof attitude stinks worse than a hippy's rucksack." Fortunately, Nicolson felt they pulled the show back from the brink. "Just as we're about to send Brandon to rock's Room 101... something weird happens ... suddenly they're on a roll … suddenly we are looking at 2007's headliners."

To be fair to the band, they had never said they were the Vegas equivalent of the Gallaghers, a band of the people so to speak. "We don't try so hard to be liked; that's not what we're about really. We're focussed mainly on our music, but it's natural that people might find us confusing."

Yet if Glastonbury was a step up for their live show, there were two even greater challenges that same summer: supporting U2 and playing at Live 8. The European support slots with U2 came pretty much straight off the back of their own thirty date headlining American tour. [At one of these US shows, a girl brought a noose onstage and asked Brandon to put her head in it. He politely declined]. Another American date saw a man and a woman arrested and charged with attempting to steal Mark's $4,500 Fender bass.

You would assume that working at the top gig level like The Killers and U2 do, that arranging a major support slot on such a tour was big business, lawyers huddled around an expensive oak desk and so forth. Not so. The Killers had been doing great business in Ireland and were selling out venues such as Dublin's Olympia with ease. Indeed, *Hot Fuss* remained at the top of the Irish album charts for nearly three months, the longest stay at Number 1 since The Beatles' all-conquering *Number 1s* album in 2002.

After the Olympia show, Ronnie and Brandon went with Lizard King's Siona Ryan to Lillie's Bordello, a 'celebrity' night club in Dublin, where they soon spotted

Bono. Siona introduced them and a great night was had by all, at the end of which The Killers were asked if they fancied supporting U2 for some shows. Imagine poor Mark and Dave – who had gone home exhausted – when they heard what they had missed the night before! Fortunately, U2 sent the band a welcome message in the form of a customised drink, named 'Bono's Black Velvet', complete with instructions on the cocktail's mixing: "Half-fill a champagne flute with Guinness. Top with champagne and stir. The whole is not greater than the sum of the parts, but the hangover is. Serves one."

"I was in the car last night singing 'Pride'. I have some lungs on me, but I cannot hit those high notes. So I hope Bono doesn't call me out for that one."
Brandon just before their U2 support dates, June 2005.

Brandon in particular was always on hand to say positive things about U2. "A lot of people complain about how old they are now but they were great when they were young and exciting and they're great now they're older. They have kids and it's a beautiful thing."

These support slots with U2 were a dream come true for the band and, finding Bono and Co approachable and warm, they all felt they'd learnt an enormous amount in a few short hours of conversation. "I saw them on the 'Elevation' tour when I'd never even played a gig," said Brandon, "so it's such a strange thing that's happened to us … To go from the heart of Las Vegas to opening for them, I have a whole new perspective watching them!"

He continued, "They're the best band in the world, no doubt about it, and they're the best live band at the moment and it's an amazing thing. We're just going to be good students." Even so, Mark is clearly proud of his own band's live show: "I think we are a whole different thing live than on record. We bring a whole load of energy and we definitely try to make every performance something special ... We're more raw, more brutal on stage."

Then it was time for Live 8. Sir Bob Geldof and Midge Ure had organised the show to coincide with the twentieth anniversary of Live Aid [Brandon revealed he was still in a diaper when this original event took place]. This time however, it was a free show, open to ticket ballot by SMS text. There were 70,000 tickets available – two million people texted in to win one. Geldof was in shining form, balancing the diplomatic global campaigner with the hard-nosed ex-punk torch-bearer like only he can. "These concerts are the starting point for 'The Long Walk To Justice'" he explained. "We will not tolerate the further pain of the poor while we have the financial means and moral means to prevent it. The boys and girls with guitars will finally get to turn the world on its axis. What we started twenty years ago is coming to a political point in a few weeks. What we do next is seriously, properly, historically and politically important." He also said, "If anyone is not going to come to our party – and it's going to be one hell of a party – they can fuck right off."

The Killers were only set to perform one song, which

scemed odd but this was not a day about egos and set lists, so no one cared. Their one song set at Live 8 was actually very strong. They chose 'All These Things That I've Done', short and sweet, but strong, with Brandon in a very stylish all-white suit (one magazine called him a

"What we do next is seriously, properly, historically and politically important."
He also said, "If anyone is not going to come to our party – and it's going to be one hell of a party – they can fuck right off."

cross between *The Avengers* and Duran Duran). The bill contained pretty much anyone of worth across the music world, including a reformed Pink Floyd (whoopee), U2, Coldplay, Madonna and The Who. The day was opened up by Bono and Sir Paul McCartney playing 'Sgt Pepper's Lonely Hearts Club Band' for the first time ever live, albeit a right bloody racket. No one cared, the marathon ten-hour day was about Making Poverty History and creating awareness. Even Pete Doherty's bizarrely shambolic and awful rendition of T-Rex's "Children of the Revolution' with Sir Elton John didn't spoil matters. Simultaneous gigs in London, Philadelphia, Rome, Berlin, Johannesburg, Barrie, Moscow and Tokyo truly spread the word globally and increased pressure of the world leaders at the Scottish

G8 summit a few days later to make genuine changes in world trade terms and debt relief [although the devastating terrorist bombs of July 7 in central London cruelly snatched headlines away from this massive effort only five days later]. Over 200,000 watched in Hyde Park alone, globally in excess of three billion. It was the single biggest televised concert the world had ever seen and, incredibly, it went ahead virtually without

> *The Killers were scorching. Imagine the pressure. No soundcheck. Go on stage. Sing one song to three thousand million people. Thankyou and goodnight Vienna.*

a hitch. By the end of the day, millions had added their names to the petition on-line to apply more pressure to world leaders to consider the debt and relief programmes being put forward.

The Killers were scorching. Imagine the pressure. No soundcheck. Go on stage. Sing one song to three thousand million people. Thankyou and goodnight Vienna. They returned to join an ensemble for the closing 'Hey Jude' alongside Macca, Sir Bob, George Michael, Snow Patrol and Razorlight among others.

Afterwards, a startled-looking Ronnie and Brandon were interviewed about what they had just done. Slowly relaxing during the course of the interview, Brandon said the day had every chance of being "as powerful as

[Live Aid] was before if not more so," adding that they made the tough choice of 'All These Things That I've Done' because it is a "positive song that fits right in." As an indication of their profile, the boy-band-star-turned-egotist-supreme Robbie Williams sang lyrics from 'All These Things That I've Done' in his set.

Elsewhere, show-stealing performances at T In The Park and Oxegen rounded the summer off perfectly and teed up the fanbase in anticipation of the much-anticipated second album. At the former festival in

"Whether it's England, Scotland or Ireland," Brandon explained to www.amplifier.at, "the crowds are unbelievable and I'm not just saying that. It's just a fact."

Kinross, they were relieved to finally get a full set in, as previous Scottish gigs had been plagued by technical difficulties and an incident with a beer-drenched keyboard. Speaking to *NME*.com, Brandon said, "We really felt we had to earn our keep today, show them what we've got – and we did, I'm so excited."

The band made no secret of the fact that they loved the UK for its support of them, particularly on the live arena. "Whether it's England, Scotland or Ireland," Brandon explained to *www.amplifier.at*, "the crowds are unbelievable and I'm not just saying that. It's just a fact.

THE KILLERS

Americans are more spoilt, we don't have that hunger for music because we can watch TV a lot, go to movies, there's so much to do all the time. There are people who are hungry for this great music. So it's a treat for us to be a part of it."

CHAPTER 10: ON A LASTING NOTE

Given the massive sales of *Hot Fuss* and the band's profile by late 2004, it is perhaps not surprising that they chose to re-release a single, namely 'Somebody Told Me' in January 2005. The second time around, the song doubled the sales of 'Mr Brightside' and landed The Killers at Number 3 in the Top Ten, their first excursion into the UK's Top Five. Not being able to knock Elvis Presley off the top spot was bad enough, but to add insult to injury they were beaten to the No. 2 spot by possibly the dullest band on the planet, The Manic Street Preachers. Over 5000 more Manics fans bought their song than the Killers' track. Why?

Unavoidably, every silver lining has a cloud, and for

this tune it was the public execution of the song by ladies man crooner/popster Daniel Bedingfield. Unquestionably equipped with a fair old set of lungs and a vocal talent to match – I know, I was dragged to a show by 'Bedders' albeit in disguise by a swooning missus in late 2004 and spent the entire night hiding under a baseball cap. Nonetheless, the acoustic version of 'Somebody Told Me' that he performed on *CD:UK* and previously on Radio 1 was nothing short of a travesty. At the very least he was risking some sort of tribunal.

Like Brandon's fave band The Smiths, The Killers seemed genuinely capable of dominating both the singles and album charts, a feat many modern bands struggle to accomplish.

Amazingly, despite Bedingfield's best efforts, *Hot Fuss* was back at Number 1 in the album charts, over six months since its initial release. Like Brandon's fave band The Smiths, The Killers seemed genuinely capable of dominating both the singles and album charts, a feat many modern bands struggle to accomplish.

"I'm engaged, and the rest of the band is spoken for. Yes, we're slowly becoming the lamest band in the world."
Brandon Flowers, 2005.

It is often the physical cost that is deducted from a successful band first – simply meeting all their obligations and gigs and PR can take its toll even on groups in their early twenties. In Cologne during their summer 2005 tour of Europe, Brandon started to lose his voice halfway through a show. The high notes in 'Somebody Told Me' sounded like he was lacerating his vocal chords and he was in obvious discomfort. Eventually he had to let the audience finish the last chorus. Unfortunately, although wisely, the band had to cut short the set. Oddly, Brandon had lost his voice in Cologne just a few months previously although that time he invited fans on stage for a mammoth singalong.

It's not just their singer's vocal chords the band might have to look out for. So many bands that are hurled on to such an exhausting schedule when a record explodes like *Hot Fuss* never actually make it to the other side. The vagaries of the 'difficult second album' are often never reached because the very process of being in a

The vagaries of the 'difficult second album' are often never reached because the very process of being in a successful band destroys the chemistry that made them full of potential in the first place.

successful band destroys the chemistry that made them full of potential in the first place. The Killers have readily admitted to occasional friction within the line-up. In *Q* magazine, Vannucci was quoted as saying Dave could sometimes be "pissy", and to his credit Dave admitted that "on occasion I've lost it. You know, if we've argued over soundcheck ... or there are days when I feel that nobody wants my opinion, that I don't count anymore, that's when I snap." By 'snap' he meant "I shout, scream, storm off." On tour Brandon misses his

"When we first started touring, it was a complete lifestyle change. We got really cranky and hated each other for a little bit. Now we're used to it. It's getting better."

Hyundai car apparently, enough to send any man mad.

Mark suggested the opposite, that actually they were becoming acclimatised to the odd atmosphere they now lived in: "We're getting along pretty well and we're writing a lot of good new songs. When we first started touring, it was a complete lifestyle change. We got really cranky and hated each other for a little bit. Now we're used to it. It's getting better. Now we've got a tour bus, so we're comfortable, not, you know, sitting next to each other in a van."

But using this as a specific example, this is probably why The Killers will make it through the mincing machine (no pun intended) that is a global smash debut album. They seem to understand the chemistry; they appear to be aware of the pitfalls; Brandon knows he isn't about to win any 'Mr Ugly of the Year' Awards; they know the rigours of the road can be brutal. This, it seems, is a band old before its time. And I mean that in a very complimentary way.

Another reason why The Killers appear to have the potential for longevity is their personal lifestyles. The lack of rock and roll excess has already been touched on and that is no small part of their apparent stability. Another key factor is their relationships. In early August 2005, Brandon married his long-time girlfriend Tana Munbkowsky. The 23-year-old Tana was a manager at Urban Outfitters, but also found time to study at CCSN college and still work the occasional model photo shoot. Their engagement was initially announced back in the autumn of 2004, which was a brave move given Brandon's growing heart-throb status. Historically, male band members have always been under a lot of pressure not to have girlfriends, or at least keep them secret. Worse still, those pop stars that are gay (Stephen Gately, Mark from Westlife) are under even more undue and unfair pressure to live a secret life. Not so Brandon. He was in love with Tana and they were engaged, so they told everyone. I guess I'll never get that meal out after all.

Tana seemed very mellow and well-adjusted to all the attention she obviously receives as future wife to one of the world's biggest rock stars. "I don't think I'd be good at planning a wedding," she told reporters when the engagement was first announced, "so I'm relieved it's not happening right away. I'm just happy to be getting married." The happy Mormon couple finally tied the knot at a private ceremony in Vegas, with few celebrities other than the band. Elton John was rumoured to have been keen to attend but the groom just wanted a simple day. A 'friend' of Brandon's was quoted as saying "he doesn't feel the need to be in the spotlight for any other reason than his music."

Reporter: *"With such a busy lifestyle what is the first thing you think of after you get a chance to take a breath?"*
Ronnie: *"My wife! I just got home yesterday and this time it was mowing the lawn. Sometimes the lawn takes precedence over the wife."*

On a rather more sinister note, the band were disturbed to see news reports about a Scottish teenage girl, Jodi Jones, who was murdered while they were on tour in that country. Later, when talking to *NME*, Brandon said it had moved him so much he had been prompted to write a song, which he initially said was about the death of Jodi, "written from her mother's perspective." It later transpired that the murdered girl had even been to a Killers' gig – the show when Brandon's keyboard was covered in flying beer. "I found it really disturbing that she has been to one of our shows. So that song is dedicated to her."

Respectfully, Brandon later spoke with *NME* again to make sure his comments were not misinterpreted or taken out of context. Telling *NME*.com he said, "A quote

I gave in *NME* last week about the inspiration behind one of our new songs, 'Where Is She?', came across kind of badly and I'd like to clarify this, as I'd hate to cause offence or further hurt because of it. I was indeed inspired to write 'Where Is She?' after I saw coverage of the Jodi Jones murder case while we were on tour in Scotland last year. It affected me deeply and got me to thinking about how awful it must feel to be the parent of a missing child, how powerless a person must feel in such a dreadful situation. The song is not a direct portrayal of that one story, though – there's no way on earth I could ever possibly pretend to know what it must actually feel like to suffer such a thing, and I wouldn't presume to appropriate any other individual's feelings for a song. Rather, seeing those news stories got me to thinking about the powerlessness and frustration that must come from losing a child like that, and it was from those thoughts that 'Where Is She?' came to be." Tellingly, this considered and thoughtful explanation showed that Brandon was very much aware of the impact his elevated public profile and fame could now have on both his and his fans' lives, as well as unrelated members of the public. It showed a level of maturity that betrayed a young man still only in his early twenties. At the time of writing, it appears most likely that this controversial song will probably not make the cut on to the new Killers album.

It's odd to note the exact moment when a band breaks out in a certain country. In the UK it was undoubtedly the 2004 Glastonbury performance. In the USA, after the time-lag where they were not even signed in their home country, *Hot Fuss* was eventually made widely available through Island. The climax was yet to come however – an early December 2004 appearance on hit TV show *The OC* that sent Killers' record sales through the roof. The show is like a *Beverley Hills 90210* for the download generation, set in Orange County, full of beautiful people, cool tunes and addictive storylines. One of the key hang-outs is at a bar called The Bait Shop where bands play which neatly allows the producers to cameo actual groups with a degree of credibility – hence The Killers appearance. For the episode in question, The Killers performed 'Mr Brightside' and 'Smile Like You Mean It'.

With two million copies of *Hot Fuss* selling in the US, the album had finally surpassed the 1.5 million shifted in the UK. American sales had been boosted by a series of dates in late 2004 with Keane, Franz Ferdinand, Snow Patrol and Modest Mouse, an unlikely bill but one that undoubtedly contained some of the year's best new music.

One Killers legend recounts a show they played at the House of Blues. Just before they were due to go on stage, a man by the name of Michael Valentine walked out on stage and introduced himself to the crowd. He told a story of how a while back he was having a meal with Brandon at an Italian restaurant when the latter said he wanted to start a band.

"Brandon, I too want to start my own rock and roll

band," Valentine replied.

Brandon's answer?

"Michael, you're a talker. I am a do-er."

Cheers then.

To be fair, Brandon finished his Pepsi, walked out and formed The Killers the next week. Now that's what I call being a 'do-er'.

In the song named after him, Brandon expands on this

With two million copies of Hot Fuss selling in the US, the album had finally surpassed the 1.5 million shifted in the UK.

intriguing character. "He's a professional gambler," said Brandon in *NME*, "who acts as if he's from the Fifties, like Brando or something." Yet he also makes it clear that the drinking and gambling that permeates this track are entirely fictitious, as Brandon has only good things to say about his talented friend. "He's amazing, like something out of a movie."

By now, of course, America was Killers mad too. Naturally, The Killers were no strangers to MTV, not since that first clip for 'Mr Brightside' blasted on to the screens of the music-loving world. Subsequently, in the summer of 2005, that song received four nominations for MTV Awards, namely 'Best Group Video', 'Best Rock Video', 'Best New Artist in a Video', and 'Best Art Direction in a Video'. At the actual award ceremony in late August 2005, they performed their career-defining song, 'Mr Brightside' and finally avoided winning bugger all again, scooping the VMA for 'Best New Artist'.

CHAPTER 11: ALL THESE THINGS THAT THEY'VE DONE

Although the successor to the four-million-selling *Hot Fuss* was originally penned in for some time early 2006, the massive success of the debut album meant that the crucial second album was not going to surface until much later. Many songs had been written on the road – having had little opportunity to write material anywhere else – since late 2004, and there were glimpses of this new material at numerous live shows. Given that since the release of *Hot Fuss* they had basically been on the road non-stop until their performances at the Reading and Leeds festivals in late August, writing new material was always going to be a challenge. Further, at the time of writing, America had only just had two singles from them ('Somebody Told Me' and 'Mr Brightside') and was only just getting into the third, 'All These Things ...' so the treadmill of promoting *Hot Fuss* might beckon for some time to come.

With the popularity of *Hot Fuss* proving impossible to contain, by the end of 2005, it was clear that the next record was the absolute priority and so the much-discussed film project was temporarily put on ice,

"We're trying to strip it down a little bit," Brandon told NME. "Not have it be so busy. Just let it breathe..."

probably until after the second album was released. "We did want to make the film," Brandon explained in *NME*, but ... we want to make a new album first and it'd be weird if we made a film with songs on it from the first album. It might be strange." For all but the most optimistic of Killers fans, this was probably a very polite way of saying, "don't hold your breath."

As a band The Killers will plug a guitar and keyboards through some small portable speakers on the tour bus and work ideas out on the road; soundchecks are used for soundchecking, not for writing and they all agree that finding the time to create new material is one of the hardest single restraints placed on them by the constant touring. The lyrics will usually come last in the process

– Mark has said that Brandon often thinks of his killer (sorry) lyrics the day before they are due to record a song. They all contribute to all aspects of the material, hence the full credit in the album sleeve of 'All tracks by The Killers', although each track is credited to a variety of combinations of band members.

At Reading they aired new song 'For Reasons Unknown' and hardcore Killers fans would have heard tracks such as 'All The Pretty Faces' several times during UK shows (this track being the only new number at Glasto). On that frantic Shockwaves/*NME* tour, a regular new song was 'Sweet Touch'.

The Killers also showcased more new material at LA radio station KROQ's annual Weenie Roast in May 2005, when Brandon introduced the track 'All The Pretty Faces' as "the future of the Killers". UK dates also saw new tracks such as 'I Won't Let You Down', 'Daddy's Eyes' and 'It's Only Natural'. "We're trying to strip it down a little bit," Brandon told *NME*. "Not have it be so busy. Just let it breathe and let it be a great song. We wrote some great songs on the first one, but these have more of a classic feel." He also said that, on reflection, the debut album did not contain enough harmonies – unlike on new songs such as 'Where Is She?' – and he pointed to a clear policy of not over-using the synth this time around. Conversely, Dave is looking to up the ante with regard to guitar solos on the new record: "I don't like playing simple Ramones powerchords," he told *Total Guitar* magazine. "I prefer chords that have more flavour. Solos aren't necessary in a lot of songs, but I'd like to do more of them on our second album. I thought we cut back a bit too much on *Hot Fuss*. I really like the solo in 'Everything Will Be Alright'. It's not one that people probably listen to because it's not a single, but that's the one I'm most proud of." Expect more of the same then.

Refreshingly, they don't seem to moan about how difficult it is to write songs when you are famous; also, from the way Brandon talks in interview, it doesn't appear as if their next record will be lyrically obsessed with living in a tour bus and how hard it is being a pop star. "If I find something interesting, I'll write about it," he told Samantha Hall of *www.rockfeedback.com*. "In the same way people like stories or films or books. I love movies. I can write about anything I want. Pop music keeps re-hashing things … it's got to progress … like … kids' stories. It's how you personally see things. At the end of the day, you're observing and commenting from out there, the outside world." The key will be if the only 'world' Brandon and his band-mates now experience is that of a globally famous band which, by definition, is a very restricted vista.

Recording sessions were booked for January 2006 and they already have had some sage advice from people who know about these things. Bono – whose sophomore album, with U2, came out in 1981 – told Brandon to spare people "the interesting second album." "He makes a lot of sense," Brandon told *NME* in late September 2005, "he's the king of what we do, so when he says something, you better listen."

"Some people don't put anything on, you know, just a T-shirt and jeans. That's kind of lazy. We just like to look good."
Dave Keuning

Given that elements of their image and sound were ultra-modern, it was interesting to hear the band talk of their next album and the ethos behind their work in terms that were decidedly old-fashioned. "When you're prolific you should put it out. In the Sixties and Seventies, it was sometimes three albums a year for people," he told MTV. "That would be ideal for us, since we love to write and play new stuff, but that's just not how it is anymore. So it'll be a good year-and-a-half between records, but the sooner the better. We want to stick around and give people good things to listen to." Many great songwriters have started life writing jingles or radio tunes, and the famous Tin Pan Alley in New York was perhaps the best example of a factory-style music writing forum. Names such as Neil Diamond, Lieber and Stoller and, of course, McCartney and Lennon are all famously prolific.

But Brandon is right. In the intense spotlight of the modern rock band, the amount of global promotion and touring needed to turn an album that sells many thousands to many millions is gruelling and sometimes apparently never-ending. Many bands just don't make it through the other end and retire to nurse their money and their wounds.

THE KILLERS

At the time of writing, the projected producer for the second album looked set to be Flood who, like Anton Corbijn, had done much work with Depeche Mode, as well as U2. Despite his recent fame, Brandon was not about to lose sight of the fact that he would be working with a studio legend. "I'm so honoured. He's produced most of my favourite albums, and I don't think that can be a coincidence," he told Planetsound. Swervedriver producer Alan Moulder was also attached to the project again. The plan is to spend the last months of 2005 writing the record then go into the studio in January 2006 to record it.

"Everything's been going so great recently, that I was sure I was going to die in a plane crash [but] it's fuelled something in me. I want to come back and make an even bigger splash."
Brandon Flowers, late 2005.

So where next for The Killers? A career playing the lounges and bars of Las Vegas seems highly unlikely. With such a meteoric rise to fame and the world's ears and eyes looking out for their new material, it is impossible to imagine a future without Brandon, Dave, Mark and Ronnie figuring on the front of our music magazines, across our TV screens and on our downloads. Hopefully they won't follow other acts that have released classic debut albums only to be submerged in the promotion and protracted growing pains of the follow-up – The Stone Roses took five years for their sophomore record to emerge. If they do, then the world will have turned a few hundred times more and fashions might have changed. If, however, The Killers put out a second album that they seem to have the potential to, then the world will have to revolve on its axis for a long time 'til they are forgotten about.

Until then, Viva Las Killers.

Epilogue

Reporter: "Have you found any similarities to being in The Killers and working at Banana Republic?"

Dave Keuning: "What a question to ask. None. There are none. Thank God."

THE KILLERS DISCOGRAPHY:

Singles:

Despite the fact The Killers have only released one album, there are in fact hundreds of variations of singles, albums, promos and DJ remixes out there for collectors. The singles listed here are the main releases, with the more interesting or pertinent variations included too. However, for those of you who are searching for the definitive list, there is a quite remarkable web site which has an exhaustive and comprehensive full Killers discography, which I heartily recommend – visit it at: http://thekillersuk.com

All listings are on CD unless otherwise stated:

Mr Brightside – Original UK Release
September 2003
Lizard King LIZARD007
Mr Brightside/On Top/Smile Like You Mean It/Who Let You Go

THE KILLERS

Mr Brightside – Original UK Release
September 2003
Lizard King LIZARD007X
Mr Brightside/Smile Like You Mean It
Limited Edition of 500 on 7" white vinyl

Mr Brightside – Re-release CD1
May 2004
Lizard King LIZARD010CD1
Mr Brightside/Change Your Mind

Mr Brightside – Re-release CD2
May 2004
Lizard King LIZARD010CD12
Mr Brightside (Album Version)/Somebody Told Me
(Insider Remix)/Midnight Show (SBN Live
Session)/Mr Brightside (Enhanced Video Section)
Lizard King LIZARD010CD12

Mr Brightside – Re-release
May 2004
Lizard King LIZARD010X
Mr Brightside/Smile Like You Mean It
Limited Edition of 2000 on 7" red vinyl including
promotional poster

This single has also been released in dozens of promo
formats including versions exclusive to: USA, Japan,
Denmark, 'Europe', Spain, Germany and Australia.

Each release has a different date depending on when the band started promoting/working in that territory.

The two chief remixes of the song are:
'Jacques Lu Cont's Thin Black Duke Remix' and 'The Lindbergh Palace Club Remix' which are themselves available on numerous versions and formats, depending on the territory. The USA has also seen many DJ remixes, perhaps most notably the 'Mr Brightside Josh Patrick Remix' – a common approach to the US where radio play is very difficult to win and the territory is so large.

In addition, radio promo CDs have been pressed with either one, two or three songs included. Typically produced around the key single release dates – thus the UK radio promos are May 2004. these will have the lead track as a 'radio edit', then often album versions of remixes also.

*

Somebody Told Me – Original Release
March 2004
Lizard King LIZARD009
Somebody Told Me/The Ballad of Michael Valentine/Under The Gun

Somebody Told Me – Original Release
March 2004

THE KILLERS

Lizard King LIZARD009X
Somebody Told Me/The Ballad of Michael Valentine
Limited Edition of 2000 on 7" pink vinyl including
promotional poster

Like many singles by The Killers, this track was heavily
re-mixed and re-issued on the 12" format,
predominantly used by DJs and within the club industry.
The main mixes in the USA for example were the 'Josh
Harris' and 'King Unique' variations, of which there
were several incarnations.

In the UK, the single was re-released in January 2005
backed up by numerous special editions, such as a
'white label promo', also on 12". In this instance, the
predominant mixes used were the 'Mylo Mix' and the
'Glimmers Mix', with the latter's variation of
'Glimmers GypoRock Mix'. The usual one, two or three
track promo discs were also made available for both
releases of this single – a marketing tool used almost
exclusively within the record industry, given to
pluggers, radio personnel, venue owners, and other key
opinion formers.

As with 'Mr Brightside', various territories released the
single on different dates and with numerous sleeves,
remixes, formats etc.

Spain, Japan, France, Australia, Germany, USA, Canada
and 'Europe' licensees all released promotional versions

as well as the key single release. Notably, as an indicator of The Killers' growing international presence, there was even an Israeli release, which was essentially a four-track promo.

*

All These Things That I've Done – Original Release
August 2004
Lizard King LIZARDD012
All These Things That I've Done/All These Things That I've Done (Radio Edit)/Why Don't You Find Out For Yourself (BBC Session)/All These Things That I've Done (Video)/All These Things That I've Done

All These Things That I've Done – Original Release
August 2004
Lizard King LIZARDD012X
All These Things That I've Done/Andy, You're A Star
Limited Edition of 2000 on 7" yellow vinyl including promotional poster

As with preceding singles, this track was made available in various promo forms as well as the key release.

*

Smile Like You Mean It – Original Release
May 2005

THE KILLERS

Lizard King LIZARD015
Smile Like You Mean It/Get Trashed

Smile Like You Mean It
May 2005
Lizard King LIZARD015Y
Smile Like You Mean It (Ruff And Jam Remix)/Mr.
Brightside (Thin black Duke Remix)
General release on 12" vinyl

Smile Like You Mean It
May 2005
Lizard King LIZARD015X
Smile Like You Mean It/Ruby, Don't Take Your Love To
Town - Radio 1 Session
Limited Edition of 2000 on clear pink vinyl

The 12" format was widely used in a promotional
capacity, including white label promos using a 'Ruff &
Jam Mix' and backed with the 'Thin Black Duke Mix'
of 'Mr Brightside'.

Other mixes utilised by the various one, two and three
track promos internationally include the 'Zip Mix'.
Further, a 'Fischerspooner Mix' was made available for
download only from the Lizard King web site.

Miscellaneous:

There are a couple of miscellaneous issues worthy of note here:

Glamorous Indie Rock & Roll
November 2004
Lizard King 1ND1ERR
Indie Rock 'n' Roll
Limited Edition of 400 only.

Absolutely Live In The Zone
September 2004
Westwood 1 Records
Jenny Was A Friend Of Mine/Mr. Brightside/Smile Like
You Mean It/Somebody Told Me
USA release only, recorded live.

THE KILLERS

Albums

Given that the band have only released one studio album, there are still a surprising number of variations and formats available for the collector.

Hot Fuss
Released in the UK by Lizard King, June 7, 2004
Released in the USA by Island Def Jam, June 15, 2004
Lizard King LIZARD011
Tracklisting: Jenny Was A Friend Of Mine/Mr Brightside/Smile Like You Mean It/Somebody Told /All These Things That I've /Andy, You're A /On /Glamorous Indie Rock & /Believe Me /Midnight /Everything Will Be Alright

Lizard King also released a five track promo which included: Mr Brightside/All These Thinks That I've Done/Jenny Was A Friend Of Mine/Smile Like You Mean It/Believe Me Natalie. This was given the catalogue number Lizard King LKO1P

Island/Def Jam also released a promo album; plus sampler CDs were released in many territories with a varying number of tracks included. The countries listed above for singles all issued CDs, but other new territories of note included South Africa, Taiwan, Argentina, Malaysia, South Korea and Russia.

There were also select Limited Editions of the album released. The two most prominent ones were in the UK and USA – the first US edition below was issued in only 100 copies and is possibly one of the single most collectable Killers records out there!

Hot Fuss
June 2004
Lizard King LIZARD011X
Limited Edition of 2000 on sky blue vinyl

Hot Fuss
November 2004
Island CG0 017
Extra track: 'Change Your Mind'
Limited Edition of only 100 on dark blue vinyl

Hot Fuss
November 2004
Island CG0 017
Limited Edition of 3000 on dark blue vinyl
Extra track: 'Change Your Mind'

THE KILLERS' BACKSTAGE RIDER ACCORDING TO Q MAGAZINE:

12 pack of Coca Cola
6 bottles of Snapple iced tea
8 bottles of Strongbow cider
2 cases of Evian spring water
24 bottles of Coors light
12 bottles of Becks beer
2 bottles of red wine (shiraz, merlot)
1 litre of Makers Mark
1 litre of Absolut vodka
Sainsburys humous
pepperoni pizza
1 loaf of sliced bread
1 jar of peanut butter
i jar of strawberry jam
assorted candy bars x6
1 pack of Jaffa Cakes
assorted deli meals
cheese (for sandwiches)
fruit bowl
spanish rice
large plastic bowls/cups (no styrofoam)
one national newspaper

FIVE RECORDS THAT BRANDON FLOWERS TOLD *HOT PRESS* MAGAZINE HE WOULD RESCUE FROM A BURNING HOUSE:

John Lennon, *Imagine*; David Bowie, *Hunky Dory* and *Ziggy Stardust*; Morrissey, *Vauxhall & I*; and The Cure, *The Head On The Door*.

WEB:

For all the official news, biogs, tour dates, merchandise and tons of info on The Killers, please refer to their official site:

http://www.islandrecords.com/thekillers/site

VAGABONDS & VICTIMS

PHOTOGRAPHS:

Photographs in order of appearance:

1a - Charles Sykes/Rex Features; 1b - Sipa Press/Rex Features; 2a - Rex Features; 2b - Brian Rasic/Rex Features; 3a - Rex Features; 3b - Brian Rasic/Rex Features; 4a - Rex Features; 4b - Peter Brooker/Rex Features;
5a - Jim Smeal/BEI/Rex Features; 5b - Rex Features;
6a - Drew Farrell/Retna; 6b - Kelly A. Swift/Retna;
7 - Matt Baron/BEI/Rex Features;
8 - Sipa Press/Rex Features.

Cover photograph by Pamela Littky/Retna

ALSO AVAILABLE FROM

INDEPENDENT MUSIC PRESS...

GREEN DAY: AMERICAN IDIOTS AND THE NEW PUNK EXPLOSION
by Ben Myers

The world's first and only full biography of Green Day. Self-confessed latch-key kids from small blue-collar Californian towns, Green Day have gone on to sell 50 million albums and single-handedly redefine the punk and rock genre for an entire generation. Inspired by both the energy of British punk bands as well as cult American groups, Green Day gigged relentlessly across the US underground before eventually signing to Warners and releasing their 1994 major label debut *Dookie*, which was a 10-million-selling worldwide hit album. With the arrival of Green Day, suddenly music was dumb, fun, upbeat and colourful again. Many now credit the band with saving rock from the hands of a hundred grunge-lite acts. In 2004 Green Day reached a career pinnacle with the concept album *American Idiot*, a sophisticated commentary on modern life - not least their dissatisfaction with their president. Myers is an authority on punk and hardcore and in this unauthorised book charts the band members' difficult childhoods and their rise to success, speaking to key members of the punk underground and music industry figures along the way.

ISBN 0 9539942 9 5 208 Pages Paperback, 8pp b/w pics £12.99 World Rights

ROBERT SMITH:
THE CURE & WISHFUL THINKING
by Richard Carman

The very first in-depth biography on The Cure explores nearly thirty years of one of rock's most enduring and influential bands. Formed as The Easy Cure in 1976 by school friends Robert Smith, Lol Tolhurst and Michael Dempsey, The Cure were one of the first post-punk bands to inject pure pop back into post-Pistols rock. Throughout a career filled with paradox and evolution, endless personnel changes, and side-projects including stints with Siouxsie and the Banshees and The Glove, iconic frontman Robert Smith has kept awake and alive to changes in the music scene around The Cure. In their third decade they remain relevant and connected, when many of their contemporaries are reduced to nostalgia packages and worse. This full-length, extensively researched biography of the band, and of Smith – one of rock's most enduring figures - is the most up-to-date telling of a never-ending story; it also analyses in depth the 'goth' subculture and its relationship with The Cure.

ISBN 0 9549704 1 1 256 Pages Paperback, 8pp b/w pics £12.99 World Rights

THE EIGHT LEGGED ATOMIC DUSTBIN
WILL EAT ITSELF
by Martin Roach

A fully updated, revised and expanded edition of the book that *Vox* magazine called 'a phenomenon' on its publication in 1992. With all three of the Stourbridge bands – The Wonder Stuff, Pop Will Eat Itself and Ned's Atomic Dustbin – having reformed in 2004, largely due to public demand, this book brings the history of this unique music scene up to date. Extensive interviews with band members reveal what they have been up to throughout the thirteen years since this book's first publication, including writing Hollywood soundtracks and running record companies. A comprehensive chronicle of all their record releases to date and massive histories of each band complete the third edition of this publishing classic. Originally printed in 1992 as I.M.P.'s first ever title, the original 'blue' edition sold over 5,000 copies - predominantly out of carrier bags outside gigs and at festivals! The second 'red' edition was released to the book trade and sold a further 3,000 copies and both are now collectors' items among the fanbase.

ISBN 0 9549704 0 3   176 Pages   Paperback, 45pp b/w pics   £8.99   World Rights

MUSE: INSIDE THE MUSCLE MUSEUM
by Ben Myers

The first and only biography of one of the most innovative and successful rock bands of recent years. Formed in the mid-1990s in a sleepy sea-side Devonshire town, Muse comprises teenage friends Matt Bellamy, Chris Wolstenholme and Dominic Howard. 2001's *Origin Of Symmetry* album spawned Top 10 hits such as 'Plug-In Baby' and a unique version of Nina Simone's classic, 'Feeling Good'. Their third album, *Absolution*, entered the UK charts at Number 1 in October 2003 – by then, all the signs were there that Muse were on the verge of becoming one of the biggest bands of the new century. Throughout 2004, they won over countless new fans at festivals, including a now-famous headline slot at Glastonbury, which preceded a two-night sell-out of the cavernous Earl's Court and a Brit Award for 'Best Live Act' in early 2005. This book tells that full story right from their inception and includes interviews conducted both with the band and those who have witnessed their climb to the top - a position they show no sign of relinquishing any time soon.

ISBN 0 9539942 6 0 208 Pages Paperback, 8pp b/w pics £12.99 World Rights

JOHN LYDON: THE SEX PISTOLS, PIL & ANTI-CELEBRITY
by Ben Myers

The inimitable ranting voice of John Lydon nee Rotten has graced far more than just the brief yet staggering catalogue of Pistols songs – not least his pivotal post-punk band Public Image Limited, whose full history has never been covered by a book until now. Rising from humble London-Irish beginnings to iconic status by the age of twenty-one, sardonic frontman John Lydon is a constant thorn in the side of the establishment and a true English eccentric. After the Sex Pistols' short career had come to a chaotic and messy demise, Lydon went on to become one of the most influential and talked about stars in rock and roll's incendiary history. This book also contains a full analysis of Lydon's television side projects and, for the very first time, charts his previously undocumented twenty-five years since the demise of the Sex Pistols. Told through exclusive new interviews with associates of Lydon, including members of The Clash, PiL and The Prodigy, this book recounts one of the most incredible stories in modern music.

ISBN 0 9539942 7 9 256 Pages Paperback, 8pp b/w pics £12.99 World Rights

SENT FROM COVENTRY
TWO TONE'S CHEQUERED PAST
by Richard Eddington

The first detailed analysis and history of the music phenomenon called Two Tone, a movement led by bands such as The Specials, The Selecter, Bad Manners, Madness and The Beat. *Sent From Coventry* examines the early years of the characters central to the embryonic Two Tone scene set in a grainy, monochrome world of pre-Thatcherite Britain. The author was at the heart of the scene and regularly found himself in the company of key individuals, and is therefore perfectly placed to chronicle this most fascinating of movements. Includes previously unseen photographs from the private collections of band members.

ISBN 0 9539942 5 2   256 Pages   Paperback, b/w pics   £12.99   World Rights

DAVE GROHL: FOO FIGHTERS, NIRVANA AND OTHER MISADVENTURES
by Martin James

The first biography of one of modern rock's most influential figures. Emerging from the morass of suicide and potent musical legacy that was Nirvana, Foo Fighters established themselves - against all odds - as one of the most popular rock bands in the world. Deflecting early critical disdain, Dave Grohl has single-handedly reinvented himself and cemented his place in the rock pantheon. This is his story, from his pre-Nirvana days in hardcore band Scream to his current festival-conquering status as a Grammy-winning, platinum-selling grunge legend reborn. Martin James once found himself watching the Prodigy backstage with Grohl, both clambering up a lighting rig to share a better view. With this in-depth book, he pieces together the life story of one of the most remarkable, enigmatic and yet amenable stars in recent music history.

ISBN 0 9539942 4 4 208 Pages Paperback, b/w pics £12.99 World Rights

BIKERS: LEGEND, LEGACY AND LIFE
By Gary Charles

A painstakingly detailed chronicle of a unique band of nomadic desperado, a full circuit tour of the domain of the life-style Biker. Trawling deep into history to detail the early town-sieges of America's mid-West in the '40s, through to the British Mod and Rocker coastal clashes of the '60s, the Easy Riders of the '70s to the Street Fighters of the 21st Century, this book offers the definitive insight into Biker culture.

Gary Charles is a global expert in his field and has unparalleled knowledge of the history and intricacies of the biker universe, plus access to an astounding archive of photographs spanning decades of lifestyle biker events.

ISBN: 0 9539942 2 8 128 Pages Paperback, b/w pics £9.99 World Rights

MICK RONSON:
THE SPIDER WITH THE PLATINUM HAIR
by Weird & Gilly

The first and only biography on Ziggy Stardust's right-hand man, one of the most legendary guitarists and rock stars of all-time. Crammed with first-hand recollections by those closest to Ronson, including: Suzi Ronson (wife), David and Maggi Ronson (brother and sister), Minnie Ronson (mother), Steve Popovich (manager), Lou Reed, Ian Hunter, Chrissie Hynde, Steve Harley, Joe Elliott and a host of others. Includes scores of unpublished photographs, unseen rarities and an exhaustive discography.

"A first-rate rock bio." **Record Collector**

ISBN 0 9539942 3 6   256 Pages   Paperback, 40 b/w pics   £12.99   World Rights

SKINS By Gavin Watson

Perhaps one of the most reviled yet misunderstood of all the youth subcultures, the skinhead look originated back in the 60s as a simple fashion statement. Sartorially proud of their working class roots, the original skinhead was a multi-cultural, politically broad-minded individual. The 70s saw the look adopted by the legions of right-wing extremists and for many years was a fashion pariah. Towards the end of the 90s, the closely cropped look has been championed by a new generation of celebrities, bringing skinhead style back into the mainstream once again.

Gavin Watson's critically acclaimed work is widely acknowledged as a classic photograph archive of historical value.

"A modern classic." **The Times**

ISBN 0 9539942 1 X 128 Pages Paperback, b/w pics £9.99 World Rights

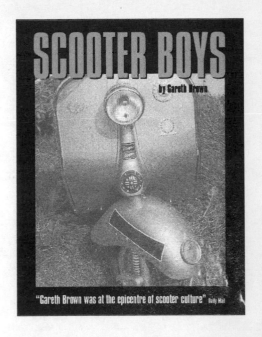

"Gareth Brown was at the epicentre of scooter culture" Daily Mail

SCOOTER BOYS By Gareth Brown

From the post-punk, massed Mod revival of the 1970s, there emerged an almost organic cultural collective - Scooter Boys. With an underlying musical focus on Northern Soul and R&B, these scooter boys developed a passion for steamy all-nighters, fuelled by a fast, absorbing and intrinsically nomadic lifestyle. They make their own rules and their own enemies.

Gareth Brown is widely regarded as the leading authority on scooter culture whose writings have been published in magazines worldwide.

*"Gareth Brown was centre stage in the rebirth of one of Britain's longest surviving youth cultures." **The Daily Mail***

ISBN 0 9539942 0 1 128 Pages Paperback, b/w pics £9.99 World Rights